Crusoe, Castaways and Shipwrecks

in the Perilous Age of Sail

Crusoe, Castaways and Shipwrecks

in the Perilous Age of Sail

Mike Rendell

PEN & SWORD
HISTORY

AN IMPRINT OF PEN & SWORD BOOKS LTD.
YORKSHIRE – PHILADELPHIA

First published in Great Britain in 2019 by
Pen & Sword History
An imprint of
Pen & Sword Books Ltd
Yorkshire - Philadelphia

Copyright © Mike Rendell, 2019

ISBN 978 1 52674 747 1

A CIP catalogue record for this book is available from the British Library.

Typeset by Aura Technology and Software Services, India
Printed and bound in England By TJ International Ltd.

Pen & Sword Books Ltd incorporates the Imprints of Pen & Sword Books
Archaeology, Atlas, Aviation, Battleground, Discovery, Family History, History,
Maritime, Military, Naval, Politics, Railways, Select, Transport, True Crime,
Fiction, Frontline Books, Leo Cooper, Praetorian Press, Seaforth Publishing,
Wharncliffe and White Owl.

For a complete list of Pen & Sword titles please contact

PEN & SWORD BOOKS LIMITED
47 Church Street, Barnsley, South Yorkshire, S70 2AS, England
E-mail: enquiries@pen-and-sword.co.uk
Website: www.pen-and-sword.co.uk

or

PEN AND SWORD BOOKS
1950 Lawrence Rd, Havertown, PA 19083, USA
E-mail: uspen-and-sword@casematepublishers.com
Website: www.penandswordbooks.com

Contents

Preface

We live in an age which seems to like romanticising the whole idea of being cast away in a distant land, stripped of all the trappings of modern civilisation. We are fascinated with the castaway theme. Think of *Desert Island Discs* – running on BBC radio for well over seventy-five years (it was first broadcast in January 1942). On the silver screen, think of *Swiss Family Robinson*, a Walt Disney film made on the Caribbean island of Tobago. It was based on a novel published in 1812, entitled *Der Schweizerische Robinson* and tells the story of a Swiss family shipwrecked in the East Indies en route to Port Jackson, Australia. Apart from this 1960 film, there have been at least five other mainstream films of the same name, half a dozen TV series, and six made-for-TV movies. And in all these versions the 'Robinson' in the title shows that the story is part of the genre inspired by *Robinson Crusoe*.

Think of the various film versions of *Mutiny on the Bounty* – most famous, perhaps, is the 1962 version starring Trevor Howard and Marlon Brando. There have been other versions, one in 1935 with Charles Laughton and Clark Gable, which slightly over-shadowed *In the Wake of the Bounty*, made in Australia three years earlier, and which marked the screen debut of a young Errol Flynn. There was also a remake in 1984 starring Anthony Hopkins and Mel Gibson. All tell the true tale of Captain Bligh, cast adrift by Fletcher Christian in 1789. A TV mini-series in 2017 tried to recreate the voyage, examining the tensions between the re-enactors as they followed in the footsteps of Bligh and his eighteen fellow castaways. The original journey, travelling over 3500 nautical miles to East Timor in just forty-seven days in an open boat, stands out as one of the most remarkable examples of seamanship and survival ever told – whereas the re-creation could not avoid the fact that the 'castaways' had a support vessel (complete with radios, charts, food and emergency medical back-up and supplies) trundling on behind them, just out of sight of the TV cameras. Surely the whole essence of Bligh's courageous voyage was that he never knew he would succeed? He was likely to succumb to starvation, dehydration, storm, shipwreck – or further mutiny – at any moment. Live with that for nearly seven weeks, and you begin to appreciate the single-minded – even bloody-minded – determination so lacking in the follow-up.

TV producers like castaways. Remember the programme *Castaway 2000,* in which the BBC followed some three dozen men, women and children as they struggled to build a community on the remote Scottish island of Taransay? Survival expert Ray Mears has made series after series based on bushcraft and survival techniques, backed up with books and public appearances. Chief Scout Bear Grylls has made numerous films and TV programmes on wilderness survival – including a handful of series of *The Island with Bear Grylls*, featuring groups of adventurers cast away on a Pacific Island.

And then there are the celebrity indulgences – famous faces abandoned on remote islands, while waiting TV cameras note how they cope with 'hardship' – imagined or real. Way back in 1971, model and actress Julie Ege did what was little more than a series of photo-shoots, wearing a bikini, while supposedly stranded on the island of Abaco in the Bahamas. Then we had a television programme featuring the delectable Joanna Lumley, cast adrift on an island off Madagascar in 1994, in which she bravely made a pair of cave shoes out of her bra. More recently we had Robson Greene in *In search of Robinson Crusoe* stranded on North Guntao Island in the South China Seas – even if the idea of being 'left alone' was slightly ruined by the obvious presence of a TV crew, a resident doctor and emergency supplies. From memory he lasted less than three hours before he had to be rescued....

Even *I'm a Celebrity...Get Me Out Of Here!* pays lip service to the idea of survival, although the worst thing that usually happens is a few broken finger nails and bruised egos, offset by a much hoped-for boost to a flagging TV career.

Nevertheless, it reflects the public fascination with 'going without' – going without comfort, going without food, going without all the things that we take for granted in modern society. The more we become dependent on technology, the more we distance ourselves from basics: a whole generation equates micorowaving pre-prepared foods with real culinary skills, and is accustomed to thinking that using an app on a mobile phone is a substitute for actual knowledge and ability. Remove the technology - will we cope? Perhaps these programmes are an attempt to peel back some of the veneer and to show how we might cope in a post-apocalypse world – or perhaps it is just cheap, mindless entertainment. Whatever; it is an enduring genre. And all of it derives from the original story of *Robinson Crusoe*, written three centuries ago.

The theme lives on as science fiction in the 2015 Ridley Scott film *The Martian* starring Matt Damon and underlies the film *Castaway* (2000). It starred Tom Hanks as a FedEx employee stranded on a Pacific Island after a plane crash which kills all his companions. In practice it was filmed on the Fijian island of Mamanuca and Tom Hanks commented that he 'wanted to examine the concept of four years of hopelessness, in which you have none of the requirements for living — food, water, shelter, fire and company'. Many assume that it was based on real events – it was not, and has a screenplay written by William Broyles Jnr. The film does not have a Man Friday – but it does have a Wilson volleyball, which becomes a personified companion during the four years in which the Hanks character is stranded and alone. It also goes rather further than most in the genre to examine the mental as well as the physical problems faced by castaways. How does hope survive, often against all reason? What happens when all hope is gone? How do people survive with nothing but their own company? And if they survive, how do they cope with returning to the modern world?

These themes inspire this book, which examines some of the real-life incidents which occurred two, three, four centuries ago, at a time before radios shrank our world, before weather forecasts gave us advance warning of storms, tsunamis and natural disasters, and before the oceans of the world were mapped in minute detail. Sat nav tells us where we are within a few millimetres – two centuries ago you could still run aground on an island which no one had ever detected. Before longitude could be measured, before accurate charts had been prepared, sailors could find themselves hundreds of miles off course. The book is intended as a tribute to the bravery of those explorers, many of whom paid with their lives, and to the men and women who refused to give up when they found themselves lost, abandoned, stranded and alone. *Robinson Crusoe* may have been a novel – some would say the first true novel in the English language – but it reflects real events, real people and real hardship.

Part One

THE BOOK THAT STARTED IT ALL…

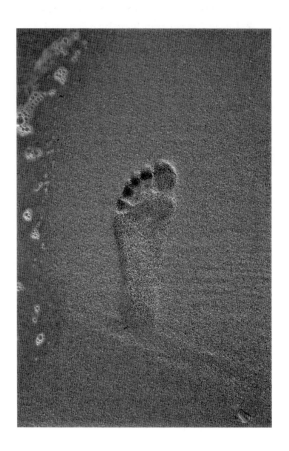

Chapter 1

Daniel Defoe

It is difficult to imagine Daniel Defoe without seeing him as a somewhat shadowy figure, keeping out of the limelight, constantly reinventing himself and regularly using different identities. He was a master of taking risks with other people's money – especially if it belonged to members of his wife's family. He was an entrepreneur who was great at coming up with ideas, and then failing to see projects through, or selling out at the wrong time. He was a man who was perfectly happy to be paid to write peons of praise about a politician one week, and then to accept a commission to attack that same person with vituperative bile the next. Defoe was variously a government spy, a Grub Street hack, a failed businessman and a writer who was willing to steal not just ideas, but whole passages of text from rival authors.

Above all he was a consummate liar, which makes understanding the man somewhat difficult at times.

He was born Daniel Foe in 1660, the year of the restoration of the monarchy, the youngest of three children born to a tallow-chandler father. These were turbulent times, when political opinions were sharply divided, when religious intolerance was the norm. Change was everywhere to be seen, not least in the physical nature of London, destroyed in the Great Fire in 1666, but also in ideas, in new institutions, in new opportunities. It was the age of the coffee house, the age of royal backing for new ideas in Science and in the Arts.

As a child growing up in London's Cripplegate, the young Foe would have learned about intolerance at first hand – he was the son of a Nonconformist and was educated at a dissenting academy at Newington Green. As such, he could never have gone to university because Nonconformists were barred from matriculating, and he could not have entertained the idea of a career in either law or medicine. He became a lifelong supporter of religious freedom and a keen supporter of the right to criticise those in authority. Freedom of speech, the freedom to write and say exactly what you thought, became the tenets by which he lived.

He was initially prepared for life as a Presbyterian (i.e. Nonconformist) Minister, but at the age of 21 he decided to follow in his father's footsteps, as a tradesman in the City of London. His chosen trade was as a hosiery wholesaler and business must have been helped when, right at the start of 1684, at the age of 24, he got married. His bride was five years his junior and she brought with her the not-inconsiderable dowry of £3,700. Daniel went on to father no fewer than eight children, six of them daughters, and all bar two of the daughters survived childhood and became adults.

1685 saw the Duke of Monmouth landing at Lyme Regis in an attempt to overthrow King James. It seemed to Daniel Foe that the movement heralded a new dawn and off he went to the south-west of England to give his support to the rebels. The defeat of Monmouth at the battle of Sedgemoor forced him to flee and then lie low. It was the time of Judge Jeffries, the notorious 'hanging judge', and of retribution meted out by the law with ferocious zeal. Foe was lucky to escape and, once the initial fuss had died down, was eventually pardoned in May 1687.

Freedom heralded a quite extraordinary mushrooming of his ideas to make money in business. He tried his hand at investing in shipping, importing wine and spirits from Portugal, and exporting fabrics and clothing. He also tried his hand at marine insurance – and lost a small fortune. He then decided that the rebirth of the City of London justified a substantial investment in a brick-and-tile-making factory at Tilbury, a venture which needed not just money but significant time and energy to get off the ground. Sadly, neither was forthcoming.

With what seems to have been an attention span of a gnat, he then thought that he could make money investing in a civet farm; in 1692 he invested other people's money in a project involving over £850 in buying and equipping premises where the civets, costing £12 each, could be reared so the waxy substances excreted by their glands could be used in the perfume industry. Not only did he fail to pay the seller for the full purchase price, but he also defaulted on his debt to repay his backers, and as a result a forced sale of the civet farm produced a loss of over £400 in less than a year of trading.

He also put money into developing a new-fangled diving bell, convinced that it was a sure-fire money-maker for recovering treasure lost at sea. More significantly, he agreed to act as company treasurer for the project, which had ambitions to recover silver ingots from a ship which had gone down off the Lizard in Cornwall some years previously. The money invested by others went missing while under his control, leading to court proceedings in which Foe failed to appear. He later wrote of his time as an entrepreneur, 'I freely rank myself with those, that are ready to own that they have, in the Extremities and Embarrassments in Trade done those things, which their own Principles condemn'd which they are not Asham'd to blush for, with their utmost Diligence.' In other words, he knew that he was guilty of embezzlement as well as defrauding creditors.

Foe was over-extended, and when the cashflow dried up he was faced with going bankrupt in a rather big way. He owed some £17,000, a vast amount of money in an era when an agricultural worker might only earn £20 in an entire year. His creditors amounted to over 140 different people, and although Foe went into hiding he was eventually traced and brought to court.

Off he went to prison, not for the last time in his career. Sent to the Fleet for debt, he must have been horrified at the dreadful conditions endured by his fellow inmates. He was soon transferred to the prison of the King's Bench, and managed – with the support of his wife's money – to be discharged, only for other creditors to emerge from the woodwork and for him to be sent back to the King's Bench prison in early 1693.

Later that year he was released from prison having reached an arrangement with his creditors. His bankruptcy was not actually discharged, but the agreement meant that he was a free man. It must have made for a difficult home life though, because his wife had moved back in with her mother – and she was one of the people who had lost the most money on the civet farm disaster. Ever the man to bounce back, and never lacking in brass-necked enthusiasm, he decided to write a book extolling entrepreneurship, with his first book *An Essay upon Projects*. In it he sought to rise, phoenix-like, from the ashes of his earlier failures, pointing out the lessons to be learned, and calling for 'projects' to be encouraged and directed towards social need. He wanted projects which would be for the public good – new mental homes, new academies and colleges and a new Pensions Board. He called for prisoners to be put to work making new roads the length and breadth of the country. He also advocated a complete overhaul of the laws relating to bankruptcy.

In all, it was a remarkably perceptive piece of writing, but it suffered from one problem: nobody wanted to buy the book. By the end of 1693 he had got a job as one of the manager–trustees for the newly launched national lottery. By now he signed his name not as Daniel Foe but as Daniel de Foe (later to become 'Defoe). While this may not have confused anyone unfortunate enough to have lent him money, it gave him a feeling that he was making a new start, turning over a new leaf. And if it sounded more genteel and important into the bargain, so much the better.

He was a fervent supporter of King William III, defending him vigorously against complaints at having a 'foreigner' as monarch in his 1701 poem *The True Born Englishman*. A witty and entertaining attack on xenophobia, Defoe regarded this work with particular pride, often calling himself 'author of *The True Born Englishman*'.

Soon Defoe emerged as one of those writers who would happily churn out articles and pamphlets to anyone willing to pay: he wrote for profit, in an age when 'Grub Street hacks' were falling over each other. He was especially critical of religious intolerance and wrote the satirical but anonymous *The Shortest Way with Dissenters* as a blast against the people in high office who 'went through the motions' of conforming, keeping their dissenting views hidden from view in order to keep their jobs. Defoe saw 'occasional conformity' as a gross hypocrisy, but his remedy – that the culprits should be thrashed within an inch of their life – was intended to be ironic. That was not how some of the High Church Tories saw it, but when they realised that they were being ridiculed they mounted a campaign to have the author brought to account for his 'seditious, pernicious and diabolical Libel'. Queen Anne took a keen interest in having the author punished as it was seen to be critical of her and her ministers. Parliament was also incensed and demanded to know the name of the author. In this they were helped by some of the many enemies Defoe had made in Grub Street, fellow journalists who were only too happy to shop him to the authorities, naming him as the author of what had been an anonymous publication.

Defoe went on the run for four months, hiding in a series of doss houses until he was finally caught. He then found himself hauled into court and tried before a group of the very men he had ridiculed in his various scurrilous pamphlets. Their Lordships were not going to let go a chance of getting their own back and sentenced Defoe to a spell in the pillory – not once, but on three consecutive days. It was a particularly humiliating form of punishment, and one where many men had in the past suffered grievously at the hands of the mob. He was lucky – ever keen to elicit sympathy, he used his time in prison awaiting punishment by penning a new pamphlet, entitled *A Hymn to the Pillory*. In it he presented himself as an Honest Joe being punished for using the freedom of speech which was the right of every true-born Englishman. The crowds loved it, garlanded him with flowers and instead of pelting the poor man in the pillory they cheered and applauded him, three days in a row.

That still left Defoe facing months in Newgate Prison – a hellhole of unimaginable squalor and hardship. Here he mixed with criminals of all sorts, saw at first hand the appalling conditions, and heard the bells which were the death knell for those sentenced to be hanged. In those dark months, when he was sentenced for an indefinite period, he became a man who was ready to be 'turned' and the man who turned him was an unlikely saviour, a man often criticised by Defoe in print: Robert Harley.

Harley was Speaker of the House of Commons and he knew that Defoe could prove a useful ally and government spy. Defoe was destitute and his wife was pregnant. Years later, Defoe wrote a description of his rescue from deep despair:

> While I lay friendless and distress'd in the Prison of Newgate, my Family ruin'd, and myself without Hope of Deliverance, a Message was brought me from a Person of Honour…. This Noble Person made it his business to have my Case represented to Her Majesty and Methods taken for my Deliverance.

Money was sent to Defoe's family, his fine was paid and his freedom secured. He wrote: 'Here is the Foundation on which I built my first Sense of Duty to Her Majesty's Person and the indelible Bond of Gratitude to my first Benefactor [Harley]'.

It was to be an enduring loyalty: Harley had secured himself a man who would do anything to avoid being sent back to prison or face the pillory, even if it meant becoming an apologist for the government, putting a favourable spin on whatever Harley wanted to say and do.

Defoe's freedom came at a frustrating time. While in prison, his tile and brick business at Tilbury had been wound up, and yet if only he could have kept it going, he might have made a fortune. A monster of a storm hit the British Isles in 1703, causing immense damage to buildings especially around London and throughout the South of England. The cost of tiles and bricks shot up in the aftermath of the storm – everyone wanted builders supplies. Defoe ruefully remarked that plain tiles had gone up from 12*s* a thousand to £6, a ten-fold increase. At least Defoe was able to make some money out of the predicament – he wrote a journalist's view of the

Great Storm; probably the first attempt to document a weather phenomenon as it unfolded across the country.

Between 1704 and 1713 Defoe was responsible, single-handedly, for writing a periodical entitled *Review*, some years before either the *Tatler* or *The Spectator* first appeared. Initially it came out as a weekly publication, but in time this was increased to three times a week, sometimes with additional supplements and special-focus issues. It was the first time that news reports moved from the purely factual, to considering the underlying issues. Defoe added spin but also put events in context, provoking discussion and challenging perceptions. Politics, foreign affairs and economic choices were emerging as matters of public debate and the *Review* was an important milestone.

Defoe slowly adapted into a master of counter-insurgency, working for the government, infiltrating opposition groups, reporting on other journalists and writers, attending meetings incognito and reporting on ringleaders and malcontents. He was Harley's 'eyes and ears', and a man who seemed to thrive living in the shadows and moving between groups without attracting attention.

Three times, in 1706, 1708 and 1712, Defoe was sent up to Scotland to strengthen the case for the government's support for Union with Scotland. This involved infiltrating various groups, including the Scottish church as well as local business groups, and drip-feeding stories to the local press with positive messages about the advantages of Union. By now he was being paid between £400 and £500 a year by the government – still not enough to cover his burgeoning debts, but enough to enable him to look to his pen to provide a regular income for the needs of his family.

Defoe moved on from churning out pamphlets to writing full-length books, particularly conduct books. His *The Family Instructor* appeared in 1715 and was to run to over twenty editions by the end of the century. His guides, looking at how households should be run, the responsibilities of a husband and wife within the marriage, how children should be educated and so on, were all set out in a readable style. In 1726 he brought out *The Complete English Tradesman*, looking at all the qualities needed by a successful businessman. He describes stock levels, cashflow, the giving of credit and the importance of keeping accurate accounts – in fact all the things so conspicuously absent from his own business ventures. Above all, it praised the contribution of 'the tradesman' to the welfare of the country. He himself was 'trade' and he saw tradesmen as the backbone of the economy.

Meanwhile, 1719 saw the publication of the work for which he is most famous today, *The Life and Strange Surprising Adventures of Robinson Crusoe*. It was followed up in 1720 by another travel adventure story, *The Life, Adventures, and Pyracies of the Famous Captain Singleton*. Next, *The Fortunes and Misfortunes of the Famous Moll Flanders* came out in 1722, the same year as he published *A Journal of the Plague*

Year. For many years it was thought that this was a purely factual account of the Great Plague which hit London in 1665, but in fact it is a fictional story based on what life may have been like at the time.

In 1724 Defoe brought out two notable books *The Fortunate Mistress…or Roxana* (about a woman who becomes her landlord's mistress in order to survive when her husband abandons her and who later becomes a famous courtesan), and *A Tour thro the whole Island of Great Britain*. The latter was one of the most comprehensive guidebooks to the country ever published, describing in detail the trade and business of the kingdom right at the start of the Industrial Revolution.

In all, Defoe may have written between 300 and 400 publications, including pamphlets and essays, and is believed to have used as many as 200 pen-names and aliases. It was a prolific output and helped make him not just the 'father of the English novel', but also a perceptive recorder of life in the early decades of the eighteenth century and an effective satirist, political commentator and influencer of public opinion. He died in poverty, hiding from his creditors, on 24 April 1731 in lodgings on Rope Makers' Alley. He was in his seventy-first year and succumbed to what was described as 'lethargy' – in other words, a stroke. He was buried two days later at the Dissenters Burial Ground at Bunhill Fields and his long-suffering wife Mary was interred beside him when she died in December 1732.

Chapter 2

Robinson Crusoe

On 25 April 1719 William Taylor wiped his ink-stained hands on his apron and left his printing premises near *The Ship* in Paternoster Row, heading for Stationers' Hall. These were the headquarters of the Liveried Stationers and Newspaper Makers Company. Taylor entered the details of the book he had just finished printing and the following day he placed an advertisement in the London Gazette, stating that the public could buy his new book for five shillings. In this manner an extraordinary book came into the public domain, hot off the press. Its title: *The Life and Strange Surprising Adventures of Robinson Crusoe, of York, Mariner, who lived eight and twenty years, all alone in an Un-inhabited Island on the Coast of America near the Mouth of the Great River of Oroonoque*. In fact, its full title on the

frontispiece was even longer, running to an additional couple of clauses. The front page also states that the book was 'written by himself', and at the time many readers believed that it was in fact a genuine and accurate autobiography of a man called Robinson Crusoe.

The book was to cause a sensation. The initial print run of 1,000 copies sold out so quickly that two weeks later a reprint was needed. Four editions appeared in its first year of publication, along with a number of shorter, pirated, versions. An unauthorised version, consisting of over seventy parts, appeared in serial form in a London newspaper in what is possibly the first serialised book of its kind.

The public clamour was so great that a sequel, entitled *The Farther Adventures of Robinson Crusoe* was issued by the end of the year. It never achieved the success of its prequel. By August 1720 a pirate version of the original book had been printed, resulting in the preface to the sequel containing a bitter denunciation of unauthorised versions, likening them to highway robbery and house-breaking.

Determined to hammer home the serious underlying message in the two stories, a non-fiction book – also apparently by Mr Crusoe – came out in 1720 under the title of *Serious reflections during the life and surprising adventures of Robinson Crusoe: with his Vision of the Angelick World*. It bombed, and sank into comparative obscurity, but perhaps shows how the author was keen to ensure that the earlier works, albeit fiction, should be taken seriously. It contains sections on such matters as 'Solitude', 'Honesty' and the 'Vulgar Errors of Behaviour'. It also examines the importance of 'Listning [*sic*] to the voice of Providence' and looks at the differences between the Christian and the Pagan World.

Nowadays most readers of Robinson Crusoe will read it almost as a children's story, unaware of the underlying themes which the author was striving to describe. The author's views on religion, on redemption, on the rule of law, and so on are passed-by unnoticed. Instead, it is seen as a charming story of a merchant trader called Robinson Kreutznaer – anglicised into Robinson Crusoe – who sets off on a sea voyage from Kingston upon Hull in August 1651.

In the book, he is first ship-wrecked and then later captured by Barbary corsairs off the coast of Morocco. He escapes, cadges a lift on a ship sailing to Brazil, and acquires a plantation there. Some years later, he sets off on an expedition to bring slaves over from West Africa, but in a violent storm in September 1659 he finds himself wrecked on 'the Island of Despair'. It is forty miles off the Brazilian mainland, near the mouth of what is now called the Orinoco River.

Crusoe is the sole survivor, but his dog and two cats are also saved. Before the ship breaks up completely he is able to salvage an assortment of tools, a musket, some ammunition and sundry supplies. He builds himself a shelter, adds a stockade and a storage area and learns to grow crops such as barley and rice. He experiments with making pottery and baskets, and also bakes bread. He hunts, manages to domesticate some wild goats, and overcomes his loneliness and despair through reading the Bible. Many years pass before one of the most powerful images in the book is described – the appearance of a single footprint in the sand. Crusoe realises that he is not alone. As he puts it: 'One day, about noon, going towards my boat, I was exceedingly surprised with the print of a man's naked foot on the shore, which was very plain to be seen on the sand.'

The interlopers on 'his' island are cannibals. Crusoe decides that it would be wrong to kill them for being cannibals, however abominable their conduct, because the natives did not know that it was wrong to eat human flesh – they were savages, heathens without the benefit of a Christian upbringing.

When a prisoner captured by the cannibals escapes, Crusoe befriends him and calls him 'Friday' (that was, after all, the day of the week when he was found). Friday is duly taught Christian values, learns English, and becomes a valued companion.

Sometime later an English ship approaches the island. The ship has been commandeered by mutineers, who are intent on marooning their captain on Crusoe's island. With the help of Crusoe and Friday, the captain outwits his attackers, and they are the ones who end up marooned. Exit Crusoe, Friday and the captain – but not before Crusoe explains to the mutineers how to survive, based on his own experiences.

The trio head for England, arriving in June 1687, but Crusoe suffers a double blow when he discovers that not only has his father died in the intervening twenty-eight years while he has been away, but that because he was presumed dead, he has lost his inheritance. Crusoe heads for Portugal, where all the profits from his Brazilian plantation have been accruing. He then accompanies Friday overland across the Pyrenees (unwilling to travel by sea if it could be helped), returning to a life of tranquil prosperity back in England.

The sequel starts in 1693 – Crusoe has married and had children, but his wife dies and Crusoe decides to set off for the island where he had spent so many years of his life. When he gets there, he discovers that the mutineers who had been abandoned there on Crusoe's previous visit have split into a number of warring factions – the rule of law has broken down. The mutineers have to come together as a group in order to defeat the cannibals, but while attempting to negotiate with the cannibals Friday is struck by an arrow and dies.

Crusoe then sets off on a journey which takes him round the southern tip of Africa to the island of Madagascar, where he is captured by natives and marooned for a time. Eventually he makes his way across the Indian Ocean to Cambodia and Taiwan, before embarking on an overland journey which takes him from Beijing to Moscow, and then on to Archangel, Hamburg, and eventually back to London. He arrives on 10 January 1705, having been absent for ten years and nine months.

So much for the two separate stories. Turning to the publishing sensation which *Robinson Crusoe* was to become: within a year it had been translated into French, German, Italian and Dutch. By the end of the nineteenth century it had run to more than 700 different editions. An Arabic version was published in 1835 and a Persian version in 1878. Over time, the book was translated into over 100 different languages throughout the entire world – from the Inuit language to Russian, from Maltese to Japanese. It can be read in Swahili, it can be read in Thai. It can be read as a children's book – it can be read in pictorial form (without text) and it can be enjoyed as a comic, and as a computer game. The story has never been out of print and it remains as one of the most significant and popular books in Western literature.

In part, its popularity has been down to its multi-faceted nature. It can be read as a social commentary, as a fable, and as an economic parable. It was even cited by Karl Marx in *Das Kapital* to illustrate economic theory. It is a spiritual journey – and it is a rattling good yarn. It has been described as the first novel written in the English language, and over the years some notable editions have been prepared. For its first seventy years the book suffered from a variety of alterations and additions, but a major step in reinstating the original text was made in 1790 with a two-volume set published in London by John Stockdale. It included both the original story of *Robinson Crusoe* and its sequel, as well as a biography of Daniel Defoe. It is a sumptuous book, illustrated with seventeen illustrations by John Stothard, engraved by Thomas Medland.

Another two-volume set came out in 1831, illustrated by George Cruikshank. He has been described as 'the modern Hogarth' and was the illustrator in over eight hundred books – including *Oliver Twist* by Charles Dickens. Throughout the nineteenth century the fashion was for both stories about Robinson Crusoe to be published together, albeit as separate volumes. The first single-volume edition to include both stories was published in Philadelphia after 1890 and contains eighty-six illustrations by J. D. Watson. By the twentieth century it became the norm to drop the sequel and simply print the original story as a stand-alone book. There was then an opera inspired by the original story, with music by Jacques Offenbach. The libretto, written in French by Eugène Cormon and Hector-Jonathan Crémieux, shows Robinson Crusoe as a hopeless romantic who runs away to sea only to be shipwrecked. His fiancée and her two servants set out to find him, but they encounter various mishaps along the way. The opera features drunken pirates, waltzing cannibals – and a dramatic rescue by the ever-reliable Man Friday. It is sometimes described as an *opéra comique* and has on occasions been dismissed as being more likely to have been inspired by the traditional English pantomime than by Defoe's work. It was premiered in November 1867 but remains largely overlooked and under-performed – despite several favourable reviews.

Various films inspired by the Crusoe tale have been made, starting with black-and-white versions in 1922 and 1927, and then with a stirring version featuring Douglas Fairbanks in 1932. The latter took considerable liberties with the Defoe plot, somewhat altering the dynamics by introducing not Man Friday, but a grass-skirted nubile young woman – called 'Saturday'. In 1954 an Anglo-Spanish version was issued. Filmed in Mexico, and recorded as Spanish and English versions, it is best remembered for the fact that the one cat, called Sam, was played by two totally different moggies – with entirely different colouring! A 1988 film version starring

Aidan Quinn as the character of Crusoe appeared, after filming had taken place on a number of islands in the Seychelles – and in a studio in Belgrade. Then, in 1997, Pierce Brosnan played the part of Crusoe in a film made in Papua New Guinea. Brosnan, who had already played the part of James Bond in *GoldenEye*, was actually about to start filming as Crusoe when he was introduced to the Press in order to promote the next Bond film *Tomorrow Never Dies* and was sporting a lengthy, untidy, beard. There cannot be a contrast greater than the one between the hirsute, rough-and-ready Crusoe and the suave, smooth-skinned creation of Ian Fleming.

A TV film made in French under the title of *Robinson Crusoë* was released in 2003 after filming at various locations in Cuba. In a somewhat different vein, the same year saw a Taiwanese production of a film called *Robinson's Crusoe*, with Mr Robinson as a real-estate broker who dreams of buying a Caribbean island called Crusoe.

An NBC TV mini-series running to fourteen episodes and called *Crusoe* appeared between 2008 and 2010, with a particular focus on the racial differences between Crusoe and Friday, and examining how they became, first, companions and then close buddies. Filming was at Fairfax House in York, as well as in the Seychelles and South Africa. In 2016 a Franco-Belgian production of a 3D computer-animated adventure-comedy hit the screens with a tale based (very loosely) on the original story, but looked at from the point of view of the animals. So, we have the story of Crusoe according to Mak the parrot, Scrubby the goat and Carmello the chameleon.....

On the stage, there has been a play adapted by Jim Helsinger and performed in various venues in North America. The synopsis states:

> *The lone survivor of a turbulent storm, Robinson Crusoe is shipwrecked on a desert island for 26 years. Though initially plagued with feelings of despair, Crusoe embarks on an emotional and spiritual journey from greedy slave trader to a man enlightened by the world around him. Along the way, Crusoe befriends a Caribe Indian and makes peace with God. This intense and enthralling adaptation brings Defoe's classic story to life on stage as never before.*

Another version, in true pantomime tradition, has the part of Robinson played by the Principal Boy (in other words, a girl in drag) and with the hero's mother played by the Dame (i.e. a man dressed as a woman). It was written by Peter Long and Keith Rawnsley and is intended for use in amateur productions. In a sense it follows on a long tradition of pantomime versions – Richard Brinsley Sheridan had put on *Robinson Crusoe: or, Harlequin Friday* at the Drury Lane Theatre in 1781–2. The astringent wit Horace Walpole was unimpressed, commenting:

How unlike the pantomimes of Rich [referring to the playwright John Rich], which were full of wit, and coherent, and carried a story….It is a heap of contradictions and violations of the costume. Friday is turned into Harlequin, and falls down at an old man's feet that I took to be Pantaloon, but they told me it was Friday's Father! I said then it must be Thursday, yet STILL it seemed to be Pantaloon!

Perhaps he would have preferred the version performed at the Theatre Royal, Birmingham on various dates in the 1780s and 90s. The part of Friday was played by the leading boxer of the day, Daniel Mendoza. He was a remarkable character, of Portuguese-Jewish descent, who overcame all manner of prejudices to become the first middle-weight to hold the title of Heavyweight Champion of the World. He succeeded against far heavier opponents because of his brilliant defensive skills and fancy footwork – and entertained the theatre audiences at the end of each performance by having a sparring session with the actor playing the part of Crusoe. Audiences loved the production, called *Robinson Crusoe: or, Friday turned Boxer*. Other pantomime productions followed throughout the nineteenth century – notably at Drury Lane in 1881.

Stars of the Music Hall were drawn to give performances at Birmingham, including Vesta Tilley in 1885. However, even Dan Leno and Marie Lloyd could do nothing to save the star-studded production at Drury Lane in 1896. It lost money, and for a while this particular pantomime faded from view. In the last sixty years popular stars (including Engelbert Humperdink and David Essex) appeared on stage as Robinson Crusoe (various dates in the 1960s). Not surprisingly, Ken Dodd starred in the leading role (1968) as did Les Dawson (1971). Many of the productions melded Crusoe with characters from the Golden Age of Piracy – Blackbeard and Long John Silver have both been known to make an appearance. Norman Wisdom, Brian Rix and Roy Hudd have all 'done Crusoe', but by the end of the nineties awareness of the racial undertones has erased the pantomime from most repertoires.

What these numerous and varied adaptations show is that the underlying story, as written by Defoe, is capable of being modified to suit all audiences through three very different centuries. Modern audiences are perhaps more likely to know the story through playing their computer games, or by associating it in their minds with buccaneers and the *Pirates of the Caribbean* franchise. No matter. They still know it as the ultimate story of abandonment and survival.

Part Two

INSPIRATIONS FOR ROBINSON CRUSOE

Robinson Crusoe and his Pets.

Chapter 3

Alexander Selkirk

It is generally accepted that Defoe was inspired to write *Robinson Crusoe* after hearing the extraordinary tale of survival of Alexander Selkirk. However, that does not mean that *Robinson Crusoe* is Selkirk's story, simply that he played a part in getting the idea into Defoe's head to write a story about a castaway. Whether the two men ever met is not known, but Selkirk was a well-known celebrity in London in the second decade of the eighteenth century, going from one public house to another and re-telling his story to anyone who would listen – and buy him a pint. At the very least, his story helped trigger Defoe's interest in the idea of human loneliness, of deprivation and hardship.

Selkirk's story starts with Juan Fernández, born in the 1530s and dying in around 1604. He was a Spanish explorer and navigator in the Pacific regions off the coast of Peru and modern-day Chile, and he ended up publishing a treatise on navigating the Chilean coast. At the time, navigators were faced with a problem off the coast of South America with what was later called the Humboldt Current. This cold-water upwelling extends to around 500 miles off the South American coast and gives the Pacific a strong northward impetus. It was a big help for sailors heading north, but was a huge problem when they tried to turn round and head south. In light winds the ships could be swept backwards, but Fernández earned his Spanish nickname of 'The Wizard' when he amazed everyone by travelling from Peru in the North to southern Chile in record time, by heading out to the West.

He discovered that the current is in fact circular, moving anti-clockwise, and his route meant that the current worked with him rather than against him. In doing so he discovered a number of Pacific islands in 1574, including an archipelago which he modestly called the Juan Fernández Islands, located west of present-day Valparaíso in Chile. The island nearest the mainland was given the uninspiring name of Más a Tierra – meaning 'Nearest to Land'. Only in the twentieth century has it been renamed – as Robinson Crusoe Island.

He rather liked his islands (there were three of them) and he obtained a grant from the Spanish government allowing him to stock the islands with goats and pigs. He lived there until 1580, when he returned to navigation. The Juan Fernández Islands are in fact around 400 miles off the coast, and in the following century various ships called in, mostly making their mark by leaving behind a rapidly growing population of rats. They also left behind a couple of domesticated cats, which quickly turned feral. So, by the end of the seventeenth century the islands were full of rats, cats, pigs and goats, all of them wild.

The Juan Fernández Islands have a very limited fauna, with no native land mammals, reptiles, or amphibians, but because of the Humboldt Current the waters are teeming with fish such as sardines, as well as lobsters. By the seventeenth century detailed maps had been prepared, and sailors knew that there was a safe anchorage and an easy landing area in what became known as the Bay of Cumberland, on the eastern side of the island. All the rest of the coast is marked by sheer cliffs tumbling down into the sea, and with a complete absence of beaches. It is a volcanic, rocky, island, even nowadays only sparsely populated. It certainly is not a typical desert island with miles of sandy beaches. It may look grand and scenic, but not necessarily very inviting. There is fresh water – and some tree cover, but nevertheless it is a formidable place to try and live. It is still very much as it would have been three centuries ago and if you like your landscapes wild, rugged and mountainous, this is definitely a good place to visit. Three centuries ago it was very, very, empty (apart from the rats, the cats, the pigs and the goats).

Those goats were to feature prominently in the life of Alexander Selkirk, but – back in Lower Largo, in Scotland, where he was born in around 1676 – he was not to know it. He was the seventh son born to a father who was a tanner and shoe maker. In all probability Alexander had a very limited education, but he was able to read – and certainly in later life credited reading the Bible as keeping him sane. Lower Largo was an impoverished fishing village in the Firth of Forth, across the estuary from Edinburgh. Alexander was clearly a bit of a hot-head, always getting into trouble for brawling.

On one occasion in August 1695 he misbehaved in church, and there is a record that he was summoned before the church elders and charged with 'indecent carriage in church'. Aged 19, he ran away to sea rather than accept punishment, and it has been suggested that he left with a Scottish colonising expedition to what is now Panama. By 1701 he had returned but was just as aggressive and unruly as ever.

He lost his temper when his brother John laughed at him when he was tricked into drinking sea water from a bottle. As a result, he beat the brother up with a piece of wood. Father tried to intervene, so he got a beating as well. John's wife Margaret tried to come to his rescue – and the same thing happened to her. Nice chap: a thug and a bully.

So, he decided it was time he went back to sea and this time he headed off to London to become a privateer. Being a privateer was really much the same as being a pirate – but you were doing it with the knowledge of the government. When the War of Spanish Succession broke out in 1701, English privateers were recruited to act against French and Spanish interests. They were given a letter of marque – in other words, a government-backed letter of immunity from prosecution – and off they went to plunder other shipping by stealing their cargo, killing their crew, taking their ships – really, doing whatever they wanted.

In early 1703, a man called William Dampier had been given letters of marque from the government. He features in his own castaway adventure later in this book, under Chapter Six, but he had a very significant role to play in the story of Selkirk, both at the start and at the end of his adventure. The letters of marque gave Dampier command of two ships, *St George* and *Fame*. This was despite the fact that Dampier had previously been court martialled for cruelty to his crew. In April 1703 Dampier left London on *St George* but even before the two ships had got as far as Portsmouth the captain in charge of *Fame* argued with Dampier – and sailed off in a huff, leaving *St George* on her own.

Captain Dampier sailed across to Ireland and there met up with a man called Captain Pickering, in command of a ship called *Cinque Ports*, with a crew of sixty-three. Pickering held a letter of marque, dated 11 January 1703. It was very similar to the one granted to Captain Dampier, giving him an almost identical set of objectives. Dampier and Pickering decided to join forces and sat down to draw up a plan to make their fortune.

They thought it would be a good idea to sail down the eastern coast of South America and attempt to capture a Spanish treasure ship at Buenos Aires, and they agreed that if the booty from this capture amounted to £60,000 or above, the ships would immediately return to England. If they missed the ship, however, they planned to sail around Cape Horn to capture Spanish vessels carrying silver from the mines at Lima in Peru. Failing that, the ships would sail north and attempt to capture one of the Manila-to-Acapulco ships, which were nearly always laden with treasure.

The ships left Ireland in May 1703 and as the voyage progressed, things began to go wrong. There were many arguments between the captains and their crews and then Captain Pickering on *Cinque Ports* was taken ill with scurvy and died.

His second-in-command, a 21-year-old by the name of Thomas Stradling, replaced him. By then Alexander Selkirk had shown an aptitude for reading charts and was put on board *Cinque Ports* as ships navigator. He did not get on with Stradling, who was much the same age as he was, and Stradling did not get on with Captain Dampier. In fact, no one got on with Dampier and the crew were convinced that the captain had failed to follow up on various encounters with Spanish treasure ships and had therefore denied them their prize money.

The privateers decided to make their way around Cape Horn. By now scurvy had decimated the crew and the rations were riddled with weevil, the water was of poor quality, and the crew were getting mutinous. The two ships did, however, stay together as they travelled up as far as Panama, capturing a few minor prizes along the way. Dampier then decided to head north, while Stradling on *Cinque Ports* headed back south. His intention was to pick up some sails which they had hurriedly left behind on the Juan Fernández Islands when they had been surprised by a French sailing ship some months earlier. They got as far as the Juan Fernández Islands only to discover that the French had nicked the sails.

At this point Selkirk complained that the *Cinque Ports* was unseaworthy. Worms had weakened the timbers of this old ship and there appeared to be a general feeling among the crew that they wanted to go ashore and wait for the next passing ship to rescue them. Selkirk was first ashore, with a small supply of weevil-infested ships biscuits, plus his pistol, his powder horn and ammunition, along with his knife and the tools of his trade such as his compass and set of marine dividers. He also had a pocket Bible, but had only the clothes he was standing up in.

To his horror, none of the other crew tried to join him. He pleaded to be allowed back on ship but Stradling made it clear that he had asked to be ashore – and ashore was where he must stay – and sailed off into the distance. Ironically, Selkirk was quite right about *Cinque Ports* because she broke up and sank a few weeks later and only the captain and seven of the crew survived. The survivors were captured by the Spanish, thrown in prison, and forced to endure a really torrid time. But Selkirk was unaware of his good fortune. He found himself alone on his island, and there he stayed for more than four years – fifty-two months in all. To begin with, he survived by shooting some of the goats, but soon his ammunition ran out. He made two rough shelters, one on either side of the island, from which he would have a vantage point to spot any passing sails – but, there weren't any.

He may well have heard about several men who had survived alone on Juan Fernández – one for five years, and a Miskito Indian named Will, who made it alone for three years. Selkirk was so despondent in the early months that he contemplated suicide. Bellowing sea lions (actually the southern elephant seal, some as large as

19 ft long and weighing up to two tons) wailed at night unlike any animal Selkirk had ever heard. Equally alarming, hordes of rats – émigrés from European ships – tore at Selkirk's clothing and feet as he slept.

In time, he was able to solve the rodent problem by taming some of the feral cats, and life got easier. Selkirk was able to start a fire with pimento wood and his musket flints and tried to keep it going night and day. Fish were plentiful, but as he later wrote in his journal, they 'occasion'd a Looseness' in his bowels, so he stuck with the huge island 'lobster' (actually a clawless crayfish). What he missed most was bread and salt.

Selkirk learned to catch and kill the goats with his knife, and would eat these with local wild turnips, watercress and cabbage palm, seasoned with black pimento pepper. Eventually he grew so nimble running barefoot on the steep hills above the bay that he could chase down any goat he wanted. Selkirk used the goat skins as floor coverings and later, as clothing, but as the months rolled into years he must have been driven nearly insane with loneliness – and the noise of those darned sealions. Twice he thought that rescue was imminent but on both occasions, as the ships drew near his island, he realised that they were flying the Spanish flag. He feared, quite probably correctly, that as an English privateer, if the Spanish caught him he would be hanged then and there. So, Selkirk retreated to the interior of the island and hid in the trees while the Spanish camped on the island. On one occasion the Spanish saw him and fired a musket in his direction, but they missed and eventually sailed off.

When it finally came, rescue was on 1 February 1709. Selkirk saw two approaching ships on the horizon. They dropped anchor on the island at Cumberland Bay, just below one of Selkirk's huts. Luckily this time around the ships, the *Duke* and *Duchess*, belonged to the English privateer Captain Woodes Rogers. By an extraordinary coincidence the pilot of one of the two ships was William Dampier, the man who had originally set out with Selkirk some six years previously. He recognised Selkirk and could vouch for his story. It was Dampier who was able to tell Selkirk that he had been entirely correct about the unseaworthy state of *Cinque Ports*. It must have been a considerable consolation for him.

Selkirk offered his rescuers goat soup and told his story of survival as best he could. The captain helped Selkirk shave and gave him clothes. The crew offered him their rations, but his normal diet of seafood, goat and vegetables made the stale and over-salted rations on board the *Duke* hard to stomach. Selkirk's feet may have been rock hard, but they swelled up in the constraint of shoes, and his recovery took months rather than days. However, the ships set sail on 14 February, and Selkirk never set eyes on his castaway island again.

Home was still a long way off though. Woodes Rogers was halfway round the world when he picked up Selkirk and ended up having so much success off the coast of Peru and Ecuador robbing Spanish galleons that he stayed at sea another two years. He did not return to London until October 1711, eight years after Selkirk left it.

It meant that Woodes Rogers circumnavigated the world, only the third Briton to do so, and the first to return with his ship and crew almost intact. During the voyage Woodes Rogers had made Selkirk a navigator while they carried on looting and robbing the Spanish settlements and any shipping they could lay their hands on. Eventually Selkirk was put in command of one of the ships they captured and on it, he sailed back to England. He was made wealthy by his share of the ship's plundered riches, which amounted in his case to about £800. For the better part of two years, he dined out on his adventures, becoming a somewhat eccentric celebrity in Bristol and London.

Selkirk's rescuer, Captain Woodes Rogers, was a remarkable man. When he finally got home he had doubled the money of his backers but was also bankrupted when some of the crew successfully sued him for withholding their prize money. In 1713, two years after he got back to England, Woodes Rogers wrote an account of Selkirk's rescue, giving Selkirk and his family a fame they had never imagined. The book also made Rogers a national hero.

Selkirk would eventually return to Scotland (surprising his family who were attending a service in the local church and who had thought him dead). But it looks as though Selkirk never really adapted to living in a community on land. He spent hours and hours in solitude in a cave he had created, looking out to sea. His family would often find him in tears, and on one occasion he remarked that: 'Although I am now worth £800 I shall never be so happy as when I was not worth a farthing.' On another occasion he was interviewed by a journalist, who later commented: 'The man frequently bewailed his return to the world, which could not, he said, with all its enjoyments restore him to the tranquillity of his solitude.'

Nevertheless, he married a local girl called Sophia Bruce, after eloping with her. When she died in around 1718 he got married again, to a woman called Frances Candis. What then happened to Selkirk? It seems that he preferred life at sea to the confines of civilisation, and in November 1720, at the age of 44, he returned to the only life that ever meant anything to him. He signed on as the first mate on a naval warship, *Weymouth*, bound for the Gold Coast of Africa in search of pirates. It would be another cursed voyage, plagued by yellow fever and probably typhoid. Within a year many of the crew had succumbed to disease, and the ship's log was recording fatalities at the rate of three or four sailors each day. Finally, on 13 December 1721, it recorded another. 'North to northwest. Small Breeze and fair... At 8 p.m. Alexander Selkirk ... died.' Like all the other dead, his body was simply thrown overboard.

Some years later, after Selkirk had died, Frances Candis reappeared on the scene in Scotland with evidence of the marriage, and of his death, and claimed the entirety of Selkirk's estate. Having received every penny from the family, she then disappeared and was never heard of again.

It is thought likely that Defoe had met Captain Woodes Rogers, and probably got a first-hand account from him about the rescue. Others have also written about Selkirk's tale of survival and in 1835 Jones Howell brought out a book called *The life and adventures of Alexander Selkirk, the real Robinson Crusoe*. 1955 saw a seventeen-minute short film made in the USA entitled *The Adventures of Alexander Selkirk* and in 2005 a book was published under the title of *Marooned, The Strange but True Adventures of Alexander Selkirk, the real Robinson Crusoe*. More recently, Walt Disney distributed *Selkirk, the Real Robinson Crusoe*. A stop-motion film based on Selkirk's life, it premiered simultaneously in Argentina, Chile and Uruguay on 2 February 2012. It claims to be the first-ever full-length animated feature to be produced in Uruguay. All of these things demonstrate that the popularity of true castaway stories will never fade.

Back on the island where Selkirk was marooned, a report in 2008 in *Post-Medieval Archaeology* confirmed that an archaeological expedition had found two sets of post-holes on the island, close to a stream, suggesting that these were the remains of Selkirk's two shelters. More compelling evidence that the archaeologists had found the shelter used by Selkirk came from the discovery of pieces from a pair of navigational dividers, which could only have belonged to a ship's master or navigator. Captain Woodes Rogers had listed in his account of what he saw on arrival in 1709: 'some practical pieces' including mathematical instruments. It is not unreasonable to conclude that the dividers had been among the items taken ashore by Selkirk when he was originally stranded.

It is important to remember that Defoe was not writing a record of Selkirk's epic adventure – he was writing a work of fiction. On the other hand, there are some very significant anomalies which have led some people to look for other influences on Defoe. In Defoe's book, the period of exile was seven times as long, and the castaway was a shipwrecked sailor, not a mutineer. Also, Crusoe came from York, whereas Selkirk was Scottish. Selkirk was something of an unthinking bully, whereas Crusoe was much more of a thinker, and also much more of a gentleman. Crusoe's island was inhabited by cannibals, Selkirk's was deserted and therefore the experience of solitude, loneliness and danger was very different. Defoe's castaway is to be found near the mouth of the Orinoco, over 3,000 miles from where Selkirk was abandoned, and on completely the wrong side of the continent. Also, if you read *Robinson Crusoe*, the impression you get is of a desert island, with blisteringly white sands, whereas Selkirk's island was mountainous, and rather green. Looking at some of the details you become aware that Selkirk hardly left Cumberland Bay where he first landed. He stayed in one place, except when he fled into the interior to escape the Spanish. Indeed, in four and a half years he never once went around the island or explored the interior.

Significantly, he had no Man Friday. And he certainly never tried making pottery – something which is specifically mentioned in Defoe's novel. Much of Defoe's work examines the spiritual side of Selkirk's hardship, such as his reliance on the Bible and his ultimate redemption. These are matters which were barely touched on in the earlier accounts of Selkirk's ordeal, causing people to look at tales of other castaways in a search for other influences.

Chapter 4

Henry Pitman

On 10 June 1689 a curious publication was made available to the public by a bookseller at the sign of The Ship in St Paul's Courtyard in London. The seller was John Taylor – and the publication was a slim pamphlet with the unwieldy title of *A Relation of the Great Suffering and strange adventures of Henry Pitman, Chirugeon*.

The man at the centre of the story, Henry Pitman, had been born around the middle of the seventeenth century and had gone to Italy after qualifying as a surgeon-apothecary. In 1685, after he had returned from his version of the Grand Tour, he visited the small village of Sandford, some fifteen miles south of Bristol. Here, he was intrigued when news reached him that the Duke of Monmouth had landed at Lyme Regis and was heading through Somerset towards Taunton via Ilminster, at the head of a growing contingent of men intent on the overthrow of King James II. According to his account, Pitman travelled south to see with his own eyes what chance the resurrection had of success – it was not his intention to support the rebel cause, although clearly he was not averse to their success, or he would have stayed at home. He reached Taunton at much the same time as the Duke of Monmouth, stayed a few days, and then decided to return home. But his route was cut off by the forces of Lord Oxford, loyal to the king, and Pitman was forced to return to the protection of the rebel forces. Events moved on; the rebel forces joined in battle with the loyalists at Sedgemoor near Bridgwater, and Pitman offered assistance to the dying and wounded. In his words this humanitarian support was offered both to the royalist injured and to the rebel supporters. The uprising failed and afterwards he was one of thousands of men rounded up for questioning and trial.

It was Pitman's fate to be hauled before the assize at Wells – presided over by the soon-to-be-infamous Lord Chief Justice Judge Jeffreys. The 'hanging judge' was in no mood to prolong proceedings – he let it be known that a 'not guilty' plea, made in the face of obvious signs of guilt, would inevitably mean a death sentence. Conversely, a 'guilty' plea would surely lead to a lenient sentence. To emphasise the point, Judge Jeffreys selected a motley gang of twenty-eight men to be brought into court. There was, in the view of the judge, sufficient evidence of 'guilt by association' to justify a conviction. But the men pleaded 'Not guilty' and all were sent to the gallows. By the time it came for Pitman to face trial, accompanied by his brother, they were both persuaded to plead 'Guilty' – only for them both to be sentenced to be 'hanged, drawn and quartered'. Two hundred and thirty men suffered that sentence, but the Pitman brothers were lucky: for them the sentence had been commuted to transportation to the West Indies – and the prospect of ten years as an indentured servant. This was no doddle – in fact it was tantamount to slavery. Those transported were simply sold to plantation owners, forbidden to marry, and kept in appalling conditions. They could be flogged severely for minor misdemeanours. Any refusal to obey orders could mean that the plantation owner would have the miscreant branded with the letters 'FT' – for 'Fugitive Traitor'.

Pitman persuaded his family to raise the sum of £60 as a sweetener to make sure that he would not be sold against his wishes the moment he reached 'the Caribbees' – in practice Barbados. Since the reign of James I the West Indian colonies, along with Virginia, had been a favourite dumping ground for troublemakers. In particular the authorities in the City of London had found it expedient to send offenders in Bridewell, especially those that were young, or Irish, out to the colonies.

Records show that between 1660 and 1718 more than 1,300 convicts were shipped just to the island of Jamaica. None of the islands were penal colonies as such, but as a substantial proportion of the migrants were convicted criminals it gave rise to the assertion by one reporter (Edward Ward in 'A Trip to Jamaica', dated 1698) that Jamaica was a 'receptacle of vagabonds, the Sanctuary of Bankrupts, and a Close-Stool [latrine] for the Purges of our Prisons.' Barbados, too, was similarly accustomed to a large percentage of its white immigrants being convicts who had become indentured servants. This was in the days before the African slave trade transformed the labour force in the colonies and therefore at the time a large, white, workforce suited the plantation owners very well.

For the Pitman brothers, it meant being rounded up and taken to Weymouth, where they boarded the *Betty* for a five-month voyage to the Caribbean. Seven of the passengers died on the voyage, and during that time the passengers were denied proper food and given no space to move. They arrived on Barbados to find that despite assurances, and despite the sweetener of £60, they were handed over to a brutal landowner by the name of Robert Bishop. Pitman complained that for food they were given a mere 5 lb of salt Irish beef, or salt fish, per person per week. In addition, they were given maize, ground on a stone, to be made into dumplings. When Pitman complained at the meagre rations and said that he expected to be treated in a manner which befitted a qualified surgeon and apothecary, Bishop retaliated by thrashing him with a cane, and then placed him in the stocks in the full Barbadian sun for twelve hours.

For fifteen months, until around April 1687, Pitman stayed with Bishop, but was then sold on to another trader. Henry's brother died, and Henry decided that he would rather try and escape, in preference to remaining in futile servitude. He enlisted the help of a joiner called James Nuthall, giving him £12 which Pitman's family had managed to send out to him. Nuthall used the money to acquire a small open boat, which was then hidden from the prying eyes of the authorities by the simple expedient of being sunk under the water. Pitman enlisted the support of two other men exiled for being supporters of the Duke of Monmouth – Thomas Austin and John Whicker. Together they drew up a list of things needed for their escape attempt: a hundredweight of bread, a convenient quantity of cheese, a cask of water, some few bottles of Canary and Madeira wine, beer, a compass, quadrant, chart, hour-glass, logbook, line, a large tarpaulin, a hatchet, hammer, nails, some spare boards, a lantern and candles.

The list is interesting, not least because it is similar to the list which Defoe has Crusoe prepare when Crusoe plans his escape in a small boat. This is before he is shipwrecked, at a time when he has been taken prisoner, and is working as a slave. He too describes a 'large basket of rusk or biscuit, and three jars of fresh water…. together with a parcel of twine or thread, a hatchet, a saw, and a hammer, all of which were of great use to us afterwards.' Planning and inventories are central to both stories.

Over a period of time all the items identified by Pitman were acquired and stored in a warehouse where one of the men in Pitman's group worked. They then bided their time. The opportunity came when the governor of nearby Nevis paid a formal visit to his counterpart on Barbados. The troops were required to turn out on parade for the visit, and no doubt after their exertions retired to the local bars 'to revel, drink and feast to excess'. Pitman and Nuthall enlisted the support of 'two lusty blacks' who brought the sunken vessel to the surface and baled her out. The supplies were brought out from their hiding place and loaded on board, and at midnight on 9 May 1687 the small craft edged out of the harbour, heading for the Dutch-controlled island of Curacao. On board were eight men, including Pitman. Of those on board, five were fellow supporters of Monmouth.

The escapees were scared stiff of making a noise which would alert the authorities. In particular there was a British man-of-war moored in the harbour. Silently they drifted past, but their tiny boat was in danger of sinking because she was leaking badly. Eventually the men felt confident enough to start baling, using a tub and large wooden bowl, but so large were the gaps in the planking that this entailed a full-time baling operation, round the clock. Matters were not helped when one of the crew lost the baling bowl overboard, and the men began to fear for their lives.

The crew set sail, steering by the sun and the stars, and Pitman, staying resolutely at the helm, managed to hold the team together for a number of days and nights. On 14 May he went to take a rest, and while he was away from the helm his replacement took it upon himself to head for the nearest land, intent on finding fresh water ('in regard ours stank so extremely'). Pitman awoke to realise the danger – natives had gathered on the shore and had lit fires in anticipation of their arrival. Pitman was sure that they were 'savage cannibals' and immediately set sail and headed out to sea.

The following day, passing along the northern coast of the island of Margarita, Pitman decided to make landfall. The coast was clear and the sandy beach looked to be a good landing place. But appearances were deceptive and the boat struck rocks. Pitman was forced to jump overboard and with the help of the men on board, who rowed furiously, they managed to head back into deeper water. Pitman was able to scramble back on board, but the sea conditions soon worsened. Pitman writes:

at about nine at night a dreadful storm arose, which made us despair of ever seeing the morning sun. The sea began to foam, and to turn its smooth surface into mountains and vales. Our boat was tossed and tumbled from one side to the other, and so violently driven and so hurried away by the fury of the wind and the sea that I was afraid that we should be driven by the island in the night.

On 16 May, after a week at sea in their open boat, the group came across a small and apparently deserted island (now known as Salt Tortuga); As they approached they were alarmed to see a canoe pull out from the shore. Believing it to be a native canoe, no doubt bristling with cannibals, they tried to pull back, only to be reassured that the canoe belonged to 'Englishmen in distress'. Subsequent events showed that this was not entirely true – they were pirates, but once they realised that Pitman and his men were, by and large, supporters of Monmouth, and hence opposed to the king, they treated them well and shared some of their provisions with them.

The pirates tried to enlist Pitman and his men to their cause, but Pitman declined. In vain the pirates set fire to the leaking little craft Pitman and his men had arrived in, hoping to show them that they had no alternative but to cooperate. It had the opposite effect, and Pitman and his men determined to await their fate on the island. In the end they paid thirty pieces of eight to the pirates for the release into their custody of a native (previously taken prisoner by the pirates). Pitman reasoned that the native would be of great use to them in catching fish and assisting them in locating fresh water. The pirates disappeared in their canoe, although they left behind four of their number who preferred to take their chances with Pitman, rather than risk being picked up by the Spanish.

Pitman then described the island in some detail – it was twelve miles long, with its south-eastern end covered in salt flats, and it was wholly surrounded by white sandy beaches. The island was well stocked with birds such as flamingos, pelicans and sea-birds. More helpfully, in the early weeks turtles would come ashore at night to lay their eggs, and Pitman and his men quickly learned to wait for them in the darkness, turning them over so that they could be retrieved in the daylight. The meat from the turtles would be roasted on a spit over the fire, and any surplus would be cut into thin strips, salted, and left to dry in the sun on wooden racks. Pitman described turtle flesh as being 'very delightsome, and pleasant to the taste, much resembling veal'.

In April, May and June the turtles would come ashore to lay their eggs ('140 at a time') and Pitman recorded how they beat the eggs in calabashes, and fried them in turtle fat, with a little salt, like pancakes. Pitman explained that 'our continual feeding on these tortoises brought us to a violent looseness which I speedily stopped with an opiatic tincture'. In other words, Pitman used his medicinal skills to cure the attack of diarrhoea, using opium which he had the foresight to bring with him.

With the season for storms approaching, Pitman and his men set about constructing stone huts, roofed with a thatch of coarse grass.

> *Our household goods consisted chiefly in two or three earthen jars left us by the privateers, some few calabashes and shells of fish that we found by the seaside. In our houses we formed a kind of little cabin to repose ourselves in, with as much ease as we possibly could.*

Pitman was able to catch crayfish and describes with great admiration the skill and dexterity of the native Indian, who could shoot a fish in water at a great distance, using his bow and arrow. Pitman discovered a plant called the curatoe – the agave – and found a variety of uses for it. Its juice could be used as soap, its fibres made good thread, and its leaves could be boiled to make a good balsam for wounds. The main stem of the plant could be heated and placed in a hole in the sand until it fermented, producing a 'most pleasant and spirituous alcoholic liquor' which tasted like 'the syrup of baked pears'. The inner section of the fermented plant was sliced up and eaten in lieu of bread.

The party of castaways desperately needed cooking vessels – without them, all they could do was spit-roast the fish and turtle meat which they caught. Pitman describes attempting to make clay pots – using sand mixed with the yolks from turtle eggs and bound together with goat hair. To his great disappointment he was unable to stop the pots drying out unevenly, leading to cracking in the heat of the baking sun. But the resourceful leader at least tried and he comes across as a most determined and capable survival expert. He lacked a pipe, so fashioned one out of the claw of a crab. He had no tobacco, so he made do with smoking wild sage. The island was occasionally visited by hostile savages and Pitman and his men were forced to hide in the interior. Water had to be fetched from a well on the far side of the island, and the rough coral and rock along the route destroyed their footwear. They had to learn to go barefoot.

After around three months the castaways saw a sail off the coast. The four pirates among them recognised the vessel as belonging to fellow buccaneers, and quickly effected introductions to Pitman and his men. He was welcomed on board as a fellow-medic by the ship's doctor – but the crew voted that whereas Pitman could stay with them, his fellow castaways had to be left behind. They were rescued soon afterwards by another ship, but this was then captured by Spaniards and they were imprisoned for six months.

Meanwhile, the ship which Pitman boarded dropped him off in the Bahamas and he then hitched a lift back home, travelling via New York and Holland – and finally reached England in 1689. His timing was excellent – it was just after the Glorious Revolution which put the Protestant William III on the throne. Pitman had left England as a rebel but returned as a hero who had stood up to Arbitrary Rule. He had been pardoned by the new regime and set about writing his experiences. He resumed his career as an apothecary, occupying lodgings immediately above Taylors, the printing firm which he used to print his memoirs. Not only did Daniel Defoe live nearby at that precise period of time, but he too went on to use the Taylor family to print many of his pamphlets and writings – including *Robinson Crusoe*. Tim Severin, writing in his book *Seeking Robinson Crusoe* makes the point that it is hard to believe that Defoe was unaware of Pitman and his story, and it may well be that they met. On the other hand, it would be another thirty years before Defoe would write up his version of a castaway's story.

Certainly, many aspects of Pitman's story seem to be incorporated in Defoe's novel. The island itself has many similarities – the white sandy beaches, the supply of water, the visits by cannibals, the rescue by pirates. And then there is the role of the native Indian who guides Pitman and his men in their enforced stay on Salt Tortuga. The similarity to Man Friday is hard to resist. Both Crusoe and Pitman attempt to make clay pots, using the same method. Like Crusoe, Pitman is constantly giving thanks to the Lord for his kindness in sparing their lives. Like Crusoe he is a thoughtful, careful man – a planner, a resourceful leader – and a gentleman. Even if Pitman did not directly inspire Defoe to write the Crusoe story, it certainly looks as though Defoe borrowed ideas from Pitman – and Pitman may well have helped mould the character of Defoe's hero.

The underlying story of Pitman formed the basis of Rafael Sabatini's book *Captain Blood*, published in 1922 and made into a 1935 film starring the then virtually unknown pair of Errol Flynn and Olivia de Havilland. It is not to be confused with the 1962 film called *The Son of Captain Blood* starring not Errol Flynn, but his son Sean.

Chapter 5

Robert Knox

At first sight the experiences of Robert Knox, born in 1641 and dying in June 1720, are so very different from those described by Defoe that it is hard to believe how influential they were to the novelist. Knox was shipwrecked not on some tiny island with no permanent inhabitants but instead was captured and held prisoner on the island of Ceylon (now Sri Lanka). Knox went on to write of his nineteen years in captivity in a book entitled *An Historical Relation of the Island Ceylon*, which was published a year after his return to London in 1680. In *Robinson Crusoe* Defoe uses many of the themes explored by Knox, along with some very specific events.

Later, when he wrote his sequel to *Robinson Crusoe*, Defoe used far more of the events lifted straight from the later adventures of Robert Knox. And we can be sure of this because although these later stories by Knox were not published in his lifetime, Defoe must have had access to them in manuscript form. And Defoe was not above pinching whole passages – page after page, when he wrote *Captain Singleton* in June 1720. By then Defoe knew that in order to breathe life into the castaway story, which he had plumbed to exhaustion in the first two Crusoe books, he needed to bring in a new character. His Captain Singleton is little more than Robinson Crusoe under another name, and is a blatant amalgam of Knox's life story, even if the sequences are muddled and reworked.

Robert Knox was a 14-year-old boy when he accompanied his father on board the frigate *Anne* when she sailed to India in 1655. It was a voyage lasting two years, after which father and son were employed by the East India Company. They sailed to Persia (modern day Iran) in 1658. From there they sailed towards the Indian mainland, intending to carry goods between Madras and Pondicherry. It was not to be; they were caught in a violent storm on 19 November 1659 during which it became necessary to chop down *Anne*'s main mast. As Knox wrote in his journal: 'being on the road of Matlipatan … happened such a storm, that in it several ships were cast away, and we were forced to cut our main-mast by the board, which so disabled the ship that she could not proceed in her voyage.'

Orders were received from the East India Company to proceed to Kottiar Bay in Ceylon in order that a new mast could be fitted. But Ceylon at this time was a political minefield. The country's ruler had enlisted the support of the Dutch to drive out the Portuguese, and in return the Dutch had been given exclusive rights to the trade in cinnamon. Parts of the island were in Dutch hands, including Colombo, but the majority of the island was ruthlessly controlled by a despotic king called Rajasinha II. He mistrusted all Europeans and was particularly sensitive to any lack of respect towards his authority. Inadvertent though it may have been, Captain Knox blotted his copybook by not sending gifts to the king as soon as he arrived in Ceylon, or even writing a letter to explain the purpose of his visit. Over a period of one week, Rajasinha's troops captured Robert Knox, his father and fourteen of the crew. Father and son were imprisoned together but were separated from the others.

Rajasinha presumably felt it was advantageous to detain these foreigners, on the basis that they might come in useful at some future date when negotiating with other European visitors. So, he allowed the men a certain amount of freedom; they were billeted on various villagers in remote parts of the island, and each village was required to provide accommodation and basic rations.

Robert Knox and his father both contracted malaria, and his father died of the disease in February 1661. Before dying, the father extracted a promise from his son that he would find a way to get back to England to let the family know what had become of them. It was a promise which was to take another twenty years to fulfil.

What happened next was very different to the Robinson Crusoe experience: Robert Knox went native. Crusoe never lost his 'Englishness' or abandoned an English view on the world. He dressed as best he could in English clothes, even if they were made out of goatskin. He never adopted foreign customs, learned a foreign language, or studied other people's religious beliefs. In order to function properly he made a chair to sit on and a table on which to eat. But Knox went the other way entirely, learning Sinhalese so that he could speak fluently, dressing in a loin cloth so that he looked exactly like the natives of Ceylon, sleeping on the hard floor and adopting the local way of living.

Yet there are common threads to the stories: both Knox and Crusoe had to face the same adjustments to their behaviour. At the start, their energies were directed at how to escape. This then turned to despair and a feeling of abandonment as the weeks rolled into months and then years. But finally, both opted for a particular way of life which enabled them to survive. In Knox's case it meant making a living supplying goods to the local community. He knitted hats and sold them to the islanders. He bought a small piece of land and farmed it; he made money supplying rice grain to the farmers so that they could plant their paddy fields – and for every sack he supplied, he charged interest at fifty per cent – i.e. by requiring them to repay him with a sack and a half of grain come the harvest.

Knox began to travel the island as a peddler, supplying local needs. And all the time he was exploring the island, looking at the forest trails, learning where the guard posts were placed, becoming accepted by the authorities for his slightly eccentric behaviour. He never lost sight of the fact that his long-term plan was to escape to the Dutch-controlled part of the island, and from there be able to get back to Europe.

The one thing Knox missed was the Bible. This is where his own experience is mirrored by Crusoe. One day Crusoe rummages through the chest he had managed to bring ashore, looking for tobacco. To his delight he finds a Bible at the bottom of the trunk, and this gives him great solace. In the case of Knox, he had been out fishing with a local villager when an old man approached and asked the villager if Knox could read, because he had in his possession a book left behind when a Portuguese missionary had left the island. Knox could not believe his luck on finding that the book was in English and was in fact the King James version of the Bible. He bought the book for the price of a knitted cap, and thereafter was able to read to his heart's content. As with Crusoe, this gave him the strength to carry on.

One other feature which unites Knox and Crusoe was their positive thinking – both had a 'can do' approach to life. They were each practical, capable people who solved problems by thinking them through and then coming up with practical solutions. Indeed, *Crusoe* has been called a conduct book, a 'How to survive on a deserted island' book. *Castaway for Dummies* would presumably be a modern equivalent.

Some have also argued that the footprint episode in *Crusoe* was inspired by Knox. When Knox finally made his bid for freedom, escaping down river towards the sea, he and his companion realised that their route could be followed by anyone tracking the two sets of prints. They therefore deliberately made double and treble tracks when approaching a river crossing, making it look as though they were a large group of travellers rather than a pair of escapees. It certainly was not the same story as the mysterious appearance of a single footprint on Crusoe's island, but it may reflect a realisation on the part of Defoe that a simple print in the sand can tell a whole story.

Eventually Knox escaped, reached the Dutch fort at Arippu, on the north-west side of the island, and was taken to the Dutch East Indian base at Batavia. From there he eventually hitched a ride back to London on board the English ship *Caesar* arriving in London in September 1680. He had been away for twenty-two years. The return journey gave him a chance to start writing up his story. He seems to have been obsessed with retelling the events, revising and amending constantly. The result was a shapeless mass of events described in a muddled order, without headings or chapters. In other words, it was not in a state where it could be published. However, on his return Knox was befriended by Robert Hooke of the Royal Society and the two men collaborated to produce a manuscript which went to the printers in 1681, emerging as *An Historical Relation of the Island of Ceylon*. It is an invaluable record of island life in the seventeenth century, but still Knox felt that he had failed to cover everything. He was determined to bring out a second edition (a wish not especially shared by his publisher) and to that end had a special version of the book prepared, with blank pages interleaved, so that he could plan revisions and additions on his subsequent voyages.

Clearly, he had not lost his appetite for long journeys. Working for the East India Company he was put in charge of the ship *Tonqueen Merchant* carrying out four voyages for the company before leaving, disillusioned, because the company withdrew the 'perk' whereby captains were allowed to make money on the side by buying and selling their own goods. As he put it, by 1694 he could not accept the company's removal of 'the Indulgence, as they call it, which is leave to bringe home toyes and small things of little value free of mults'.

Those four voyages for the East India Company were not without incident. On the first voyage, the *Tonqueen Merchant* sailed to Tonkin in what is now North Vietnam before returning to Batavia with a cargo of 'very rich goods as wrought silks and Muske and … lacquered wares.' But to the great dismay of Knox, the Company's agent decided that the little ship was not best suited to complete the return leg with such a valuable cargo, and he was ordered to transfer everything to the much larger and better defended ship the *Surat Merchant*. She carried thirty cannon and had a crew three times larger than *Tonqueen Merchant*, but it meant that Knox was left to carry a low-value cargo of a type of wood – a cinnamon substitute – for the return leg. The irony is that whereas *Tonqueen Merchant* came home unscathed, Knox was to write: 'the 'Great Ship, the *Surat Merchant*, which was intrusted with all the rich goods I had brought from Tonqueene Perished by the way home with all her men, and was never since heard of.'

For the next trip the East India Company decided to refit the *Tonqueen Merchant* by cutting her in half and adding an extra section, making her 12 ft longer. Knox was not informed of the reason, but when he received his sailing orders all became clear: his vessel was now a slaving ship, and his orders were to proceed to Madagascar, purchase 250 slaves, and then return via the Cape of Good Hope before heading to the remote island of St Helena. There, the Company were sure that they would find a ready market for the human cargo.

The irony is that when Knox reached Madagascar he was confronted by almost the identical set of circumstances which had led to his capture in Ceylon. The ship was caught in a violent storm, and in an effort to stop her capsizing the decision was made to hack down the mainmast with an axe. The stricken vessel then made landfall, and Knox started negotiations for the acquisition of the slaves belonging to the local ruler. Yet again, he was tricked into coming ashore personally and was immediately held captive by the local ruler who demanded guns, ammunition – and brandy. Eventually Knox and his men managed to escape, but had only been able to purchase fifty slaves, a far from profitable number. The mainmast was replaced with the mizzenmast, and off he sailed to St Helena. Here he had to be carried ashore in his hammock suffering greatly from an attack of scurvy which laid him low for weeks on end. By May 1685 he had finally recovered sufficiently to be ready to commence the return leg to England, only to watch in disbelief as his crew cut the ropes and sailed off into the distance, leaving Knox on shore. They had not only stolen his ship, they had also taken with them that most valuable cargo of all – Knox's manuscript. The mutineers also had with them the proceeds of sale of the fifty slaves, leaving Knox with nothing except the clothes on his back. Once more, he found himself cast away, not knowing whether he would be stranded for weeks, months or even years. St Helena was, and indeed still is, one of the most remote islands in the entire world.

In the event his sojourn ended in September when the ship *Caesar* called in to the main harbour. By a remarkable coincidence this was the same ship, under the command of the same captain, which had been involved in the return voyage from Batavia four years earlier, when Knox first escaped from Ceylon.

Another coincidence followed when *Caesar* reached Plymouth; who should be in harbour but the *Tonqueen Merchant*. Knox naturally recognised his old ship, even though it bore a new name (*Greyhound*), but by then the mutineers had guessed that the new arrival would have their old captain on board, so they fled aboard *Greyhound*, abandoning her off Cowes on the Isle of Wight. After a short delay, news reached Knox that he was to proceed to Cowes and regain possession of his ship, and to his great joy he discovered that the one and only thing left behind by the mutineers … was the manuscript. It was, however, a difficult return. The East India Company held a further enquiry into the mutiny, and Knox stood accused of giving his men 'scant allowance of provisions'. There seemed to be the feeling that whereas he, Knox, 'had been brought up in Slavery and could live upon turnip-tops', he had kept the men on short rations.

He was however exonerated from blame and the company decided to send Knox on another voyage on *Tonqueen Merchant*, this time as a privateer. In other words, he had the benefit of a letter of marque and had been given the job of raiding and looting the property of the Great Mughal in India. This 'legalised piracy' suited Knox because he had little capital with which to buy goods to trade and he saw the venture as an opportunity to raise his 'decayed fortune'. In practice he managed to capture a single ship belonging to the Indian ruler, taking it to Persia. When he sailed back towards India and the north western state of Sindh, he had the misfortune to be caught in the unpredictable currents of the area. Having anchored his ship he sent a longboat ashore with eight men. He waited eight days for them to return, and then gave up waiting and sailed off, leaving the men to an unknown fate. Ill-fortune dogged his return, with bad storms forcing him to spend the entire winter stranded on Mauritius. Worse followed, with the ship developing a bad leak on the leg back to England. Knox was forced to divert across the Atlantic to Barbados to effect repairs and as a result, he did not get back home until 1689. Early the following year, he embarked again on a slaving trip, again to Madagascar, but this time en route to Sumatra. On this occasion he managed to avoid being caught and taken prisoner while purchasing the slaves, and the voyage proved to be profitable. Knox sold the slaves and bought a cargo of pepper, getting back to England in 1694.

He returned to enjoy some of the fruits of the fame which his book had brought him. Some eleven years earlier he been granted an audience by Charles II and had entertained the king and his courtiers with stories of his capture and escape. His book had been translated into German in 1689, Dutch in 1692 and into French in 1693, so by now he was internationally famous. It made him even more determined to finish revising and extending his autobiography and the next two years were entirely taken up with literary matters. His plan was to bring out a second edition of his *Historical Relation* as well as a separate book on his subsequent adventures, but the publisher baulked at the length and rambling nature of the project.

Eventually he tired of hanging around London working on his manuscripts and decided to go back to sea for what was to be his final voyage. This was a venture which was independent of the East India Company and involved the newly built merchant vessel *Mary*. The voyage was a commercial failure, although it did have the piquancy of requiring Knox to land once more in Ceylon. Knox returned home poorer than when he left and retired from the sea in 1701. He still nursed ambitions to publish a sequel to his *An Historical Relation* and his manuscript was hawked around a number of third parties in the hope that a publisher could be found. It is quite possible that Defoe read the revised manuscript at this time, which would explain why large chunks of it reappeared in *Captain Singleton*, which came out in print just three weeks before Knox died in June 1720.

Defoe has Singleton taking part in a mutiny in Madagascar, inspired by the short rations on which the crew had been kept (shades of St Helena...). He then gets stranded on the same stretch of Madagascan coast as Knox and settles there in a way which mirrors Knox's life as a captive in Ceylon. He then sets off on a journey to cross Africa on foot, echoing some of the experiences described by Knox when he planned his escape through the forests and mountains of Ceylon, albeit on a different scale. Defoe's Singleton then emulates Knox by trying his hand as a slave-trader and as a pirate before eventually returning to London, repenting of his wicked past, and settling down to a contented married life. In this respect at least, Singleton departs from his alter ego Robert Knox, who never married. But many of the descriptions of shipwrecks, mutinies, privations and melees are lifted straight from Knox's own autobiography.

The manuscripts which Knox intended for publication ended up many years later in the Bodleian Library, uncatalogued and unnoticed for nearly two centuries. It took a massive amount of research and numerous false starts before the full second edition of *An Historical Relation* came out in print as a two-volume book which included the autobiography. It is a monument to the tenacity of one man, J. H. O. Paulusz, who spent sixty years collating and editing the work, as well as preparing a preface which ran to some 500 pages. It was published in 1989 – a mere 269 years after Knox had died.

Chapter 6

William Dampier

One other person whose life story almost certainly influenced Defoe was the explorer William Dampier. He had been born in 1651 and by the end of the 1600s was one of the most famous mariners alive. Nowadays in Britain he is almost totally forgotten. In Yeovil, the nearest town to where he was born (East Coker) there is a Dampier Street and in the port of Bristol there is a Dampier Road – but apart from that, virtually nothing. True, in the southern hemisphere there is a city and major port named after him, along with an island, an archipelago, a mountain and an ocean ridge. But in his homeland, he is overlooked. Not so in the early 1700s when he was revered for having sailed around the world not once or twice, but three times. That has to be seen in the context that very few Englishmen had ever performed the feat – one of them being Sir Francis Drake.

He was famous for having been a pirate, for being an intrepid explorer, and for writing a book entitled *A New Voyage Round the World*. This inspired the public with tales of far-off lands, inhabited by exotic painted (i.e. tattooed) natives, with strange animals and unknown flora. His book influenced many other travel writers with his accurate descriptions of a fantastical new world, and in so doing he introduced dozens of words to the English language. Some he probably invented – such as 'sub-species' and 'subsistence farming' – while others he simply brought in from foreign languages (such as cashew, barbecue, avocado and soy sauce). You only have to look at his descriptions of strange birds and other wildlife to see how Defoe was inspired to write about penguins and seals inhabiting the Caribbean island on which he placed Crusoe. Defoe may not have got it right about the penguins, but it served the public appetite for the exotic!

Later, Dampier was to inspire Charles Darwin with his observation that the green back turtles in the Galapagos differed from their counterparts in the Caribbean (as a result of different environmental conditions). He similarly influenced the German oceanographer and hydrographer Alexander von Humboldt because of his notes on winds and ocean currents. He was a man with an insatiable appetite for new things; he was 'a sailor's sailor', and in many ways the character of Robinson Crusoe mirrors that of William Dampier – far more so than the prickly Scot Selkirk.

There are certain instances where Dampier's life may have had a direct influence on Defoe. The first is the fact that Dampier was himself a castaway, along with the fifty crew on board the naval ship *Roebuck*, when it sank off Ascension Island on 21 February 1701. Dampier was to describe his experiences in his book entitled *A voyage to New Holland* and it quickly became a publishing sensation.

Some understanding of what it must have been like on Ascension Island comes from a description written nearly a century later by George Maxwell. Writing in 1793, he stated:

Ascension is an uninhabited island about 20 miles in circumference. Composed of porous rock, calcined earth and pumice stone, the surface in general powdered as it were with sulphur, and hot vitriolic fumes pouring from the mountains destroying all vegetation. Not a blade of grass to be seen, though there are many wild goats; these may possibly have reservoirs of water and hardy plants to glean on the windward side where the destructive vapours cannot reach. The bay abounds with fish, particularly a small cod, but they have a black appearance, and when dead grow putrid remarkably soon, which should deter people from using them, as many have experienced their deleterious effects. Vessels bound for English Road should run down on the North Side, and take Pelican Point within two cable length, being a steep rocky shore, then brace up to fetch in with the bay, which they may easily do, to anchoring ground, the first stretch within one third of a mile of the beach, in 10 or 12 fathom water, fine sandy bottom, bringing the flagstaff on Constitution Hill to bear S.E.

Maxwell continued:

There is another bay under the south about two miles from Rat Corner, called French Road, and better frequented by turtle, but lies very open to the sea, and is dangerous for boats on account of its rocky beach and heavy surf. Vessels calling at

Ascension for turtle often turn 50 in a night, from 3cwt to 5cwt each, and may be found in great abundance 8 months out of 12, say June, July, August and September excepted, when the season is too cold. They are wholesome, nutritious food, and prove a salutary refreshment to mariners on long voyages. It would therefore be a good maxim for vessels leaving the coast of Angola, with the wind at S.S.E or even at S.W to call at the island, being little or nothing out of their course to the West Indies, and would most assuredly be of infinite service, in correcting that putrid scorbutic habit, which prevails more or less on board of African ships especially if those concerned in that trade were to erect a few houses for the accommodation of the sick on shore, until the vessel is properly aired and fumigated, the turtle taken on board, and they might also have a supply of water, if cisterns were constructed for that purpose, as it might be done at a very moderate expense.

In other words, there were lots of turtles and there were wild goats, but the landscape was volcanic and forbidding. As a later island commander remarked: 'This is one of the strangest places on the face of the earth'.

Dampier did not have the luxury of following George Maxwell's advice about suitable landing points. He was sailing north from Cape Town, heading for England, when it became clear that the leaking old tub *Roebuck* was never going to make it home. Affected by worm, the timbers were porous. A bad leak had developed and the only person qualified to carry out remedial work was the carpenter's mate. He came up with the questionable suggestion that the way to cure the leak was to cut out some of the principal timbers. Alarmed, Dampier insisted that before work was undertaken, the men should first have spare timbers etc. in place, ready to fill the hole. In Dampier's own words:

The carpenter's mate, gunner, and boatswain went down; and soon after I followed them myself and asked them whether they could come at the leak: they said they believed they might, but cutting the ceiling; I told the carpenter's mate (who was the only person in the ship that understood anything of carpenter's work) that if he thought he could come at the leak by cutting the ceiling without weakening the ship he might do it, for he had stopped one leak so before; which though not so big as this, yet, having seen them both, I thought he might as well do this as the other. Wherefore I left him to do his best.

The ceiling being cut, they could not come at the leak…. I went down again to see it, and found the water to come in very violently. I told them I never had known any such thing as cutting timbers to stop leaks; but if they who ought to be best judges in such cases thought they could do any good I bid them use their utmost care and diligence, promising the carpenter's mate that I would always be a friend to him

if he could and would stop it: he said by 4 o'clock in the afternoon he would make
all well, it being then about 11 in the forenoon. In the afternoon my men were all
employed, pumping with both pumps; except such as assisted the carpenter's mate.

To get to the leak the powder room had to be emptied first. The ship had accordingly moored off Clarence Bay in the north west of Ascension Island, while the men laboured on the pumps. When the carpenter's mate thought that he had identified the problem, and started to cut away one of the main ribs of the ship to get at the affected area, water started to flood in.

Dampier's own description of the events is worth recording:

About one in the afternoon I went down again and the carpenter's mate was cutting
the after-part of the timber over the leak. Some said it was best to cut the timber
away at once; I bid them hold their tongue and let the carpenter's mate alone; for
he knew best and I hoped he would do his utmost to stop the leak. I desired him
to get everything ready for stopping the violence of the water, before he cut any
further; for fear it should overpower us at once. I had already ordered the carpenter
to bring all the oakum he had, and the boatswain to bring all the waste cloths to
stuff in upon occasion; and had for the same purpose sent down my own bedclothes.
The carpenter's mate said he should want short stanchions to be placed so that the
upper end should touch the deck, and the under-part rest on what was laid over the
leak; and presently took a length for them. I asked the master-carpenter what he
thought best to be done: he replied till the leak was all open, he could not tell. Then
he went away to make a stanchion, but it was too long: I ordered him to make many
of several lengths, that we might not want of any size. So once more desiring the
carpenter's mate to use his utmost endeavours I went up, leaving the boatswain and
some others there.

Dampier's frustration turned to despair:

About 5 o'clock the boatswain came to me and told me the leak was increased,
and that it was impossible to keep the ship above water; when on the contrary I
expected to have had the news of the leak's being stopped. I presently went down
and found the timber cut away, but nothing in readiness to stop the force of the
water from coming in. I asked them why they would cut the timber before they had
got all things in readiness: the carpenter's mate answered they could do nothing till
the timber was cut that he might take the dimensions of the place; and that there
was a caulk which he had lined out, preparing by the carpenter's boy. I ordered
them in the meantime to stop in oakum, and some pieces of beef; which accordingly

was done, but all to little purpose: for now the water gashed in with such violence, notwithstanding all our endeavours to check it, that it flew in over the ceiling; and for want of passage out of the room overflowed it above two foot deep.

Further timbers had to be cut to allow the incoming waters to run off safely and for a while the men worked tirelessly on the chain pumps, as well as baling by hand, to try and stem the tide. However, the result was a foregone conclusion – they had to abandon ship.

I ordered the bulkhead be cut open, to give passage to the water that it might drain out of the room; and withal ordered to clear away abaft [i.e. behind] the bulkhead, that we might bail: so now we had both pumps going and as many bailing as could; and by this means the water began to decrease; which gave me some hope of saving the ship. I asked the carpenter's mate what he thought of it; he said 'Fear not; for by 10 o'clock at night I'll engage to stop the leak.' I went from him with a heavy heart; but, putting a good countenance upon the matter, encouraged my men, who pumped and bailed very briskly; and when I saw occasion I gave them some drams to comfort them. About 11 o'clock at night the boatswain came to me and told me that the leak still increased; and that the plank was so rotten it broke away like dirt; and that now it was impossible to save the ship; for they could not come at the leak because the water in the room was got above it.

For Dampier there was no panic but an orderly decision to abandon the ship, first taking with him all his journals and charts which he had been working on during his voyage to explore the coast of what is now Australia, and back via Sumatra. He also removed water casks, a supply of food, and cut some of the sails for use as a shelter on land. He immediately set about exploring this barren land.

As he wrote in his book:

On the 26th following we, to our great comfort, found a spring of fresh water about 8 miles from our tents, beyond a very high mountain which we must pass over: so that now we were, by God's Providence, in a condition of subsisting some time; having plenty of very good turtle by our tents, and water for the fetching. The next day I went up to see the watering-place, accompanied with most of my officers. We lay by the way all night and next morning early got thither; where we found a very fine spring on the south-east side of the high mountain, about half a mile from its top: but the continual fogs make it so cold here that it is very unwholesome living by the water. Near this place are abundance of goats and land-crabs.

Ironically, there are only two supplies of fresh water on the island and the one which is nowadays known as 'Dampiers Drip' is almost certainly *not* the spring which Dampier's men discovered. Indeed, it is far more likely that 'Dampiers Drip' is the rather insignificant supply of water located by that other castaway on Ascension Island, Leendert Hasenbosch, referred to in Chapter Fourteen. The description of the supply in Dampier's book, and the fact that it was sufficient to supply fifty men on an open-ended basis, makes it much more likely that Dampier was referring to fresh water in an area now known as Breakneck Valley.

The point worth emphasising is this: Dampier had ensured that his men had shelter, fresh water and a plentiful supply of meat. Not for them any soul-searching or feeling of abandonment, starvation and impending death. They simply waited until they were rescued. In all, the fifty men stayed for around six weeks. At one point they located a group of four trees, one of which had a trunk into which an earlier visitor had carved the date '1642'. For them, it must have been a 'footprint in the sand' moment.

Dampier noted that:

About half a furlong from these we found a convenient place for sheltering men in any weather. Hither many of our men resorted; the hollow rocks affording convenient lodging; the goats, land-crabs, men-of-war-birds and boobies good food; and the air was here exceeding wholesome.

As it happened the first ships to be sighted did not call in at the island, but sailed straight past, just about one week after *Roebuck* had landed. The men had thought that rescue was imminent and had rounded up over twenty turtles in order to give a welcoming supper to their rescuers. Dampier noted the fact that the ships simply sailed past and so he ordered the release of the turtles. He continued his narrative:

Here we continued without seeing any other ship till the second of April; when we saw eleven sail to windward of the island: but they likewise passed by. The day after appeared four sail, which came to anchor in this bay. They were His Majesty's ships the Anglesey, Hastings and Lizard; and the Canterbury East India ship. I went on board the Anglesey with about thirty-five of my men; and the rest were disposed of into the other two men-of-war.

Dampier was well aware of his good fortune at being rescued without any loss of crew, writing in his journal:

For which wonderful deliverance from so many and great dangers I think myself bound to return continual thanks to Almighty God; whose divine providence if it shall please to bring me safe again to my native country from my present intended voyage; I hope to publish a particular account of all the material things I observed in the several places which I have now but barely mentioned.

He did indeed publish his account, as *A continuation of a Voyage to New Holland* in 1703. It gave sensational details not just of his shipwreck and recovery, but also of his earlier discoveries on board *Roebuck* off Shark Bay in what is now Australia, and around the coast of Papua New Guinea. The public were enthralled.

Dampier had returned to England only to find that he had to face a court martial, accused of cruelty to his lieutenant George Fisher, caned, and later sent to prison in Bahia (Brazil). The two men had been fighting and bickering constantly during the first part of the voyage and Dampier probably reckoned that leaving the lieutenant to kick his heels in prison was the best way of ensuring morale among the rest of the crew. But on his release George Fisher; who had influential friends in high places, petitioned the Admiralty. The trial took place in June 1702. Whereas Dampier was exonerated of all blame for the loss of *Roebuck*, he was convicted of 'cruel usage of Lieutenant Fisher' and deemed unfit to serve in the navy. In particular it was ordered that he should never be given command of a Royal Navy vessel ever again. The episode must have caused Dampier much annoyance: he had been made to forfeit his naval pay for the whole three years of the voyage on board *Roebuck*, as well as having to live with the ignominy of losing a ship under his command.

Despite the verdict against him, the Admiralty still held Dampier in high-regard. When war broke out with Spain the following year, Dampier was immediately given command of another naval vessel, *St George* and given letters of marque enabling him to set off round Cape Horn on a mission to sack Spanish settlements and to seize any Spanish merchant ships off the coast of South America. As described already, it was on this voyage, accompanying *Cinque Ports*, that Alexander Selkirk had been marooned on the Juan Fernández Islands.

As an aside, the wreck of *Roebuck* is believed to have been discovered in 2001 in 15 ft of water, 100 yards off-shore from Long Beach in Clarence Bay. Finds included a ship's bell bearing an engraved broad arrow (the symbol of government property) whereas no other naval ships are known to have gone down in that area. Also recovered was a grappling anchor – specifically mentioned by Dampier's rescuers as having been left behind – and a giant clam-shell. At first sight this may not appear to be the most reliable of identifying finds, but in fact it is pretty conclusive: such shells are never found in the Atlantic Ocean; on the other hand, it is known from Dampier's journals that he was bringing samples of giant clam-shells back with him on board *Roebuck* and that these went down with the ship. There is no other logical explanation for these finds: they can only have come from *Roebuck*.

There are other aspects of Dampier's various voyages which justify comparison with Defoe's masterpiece, one of which centres on Jeoly (or Giolo), a native of the island of Miangas – now in Indonesia. In all probability he had been a warrior, covered in tattoos recording his bravery in battle. He had been captured and enslaved before being sold to Dampier, who then brought him back to London. The pair shared numerous adventures, and a mutual respect emerged between them. However, Dampier was desperate for money and decided to exhibit 'Prince Jeoly' at various 'shows' in London and its environs, apparently intending to return Jeoly to his homeland once enough money had been raised. In practice Dampier was conned out of control of Jeoly by merchants to whom he owed money. They took Jeoly and exhibited him in a series of freak shows at the *Blue Boar's Head Inn* in Fleet Street and later Oxford.

The word 'tattoo' was not at that stage in general use – Jeoly was simply referred to as the 'painted prince', with his body decorated from head to foot in swirls, patterns and geometric lines. Dampier described his appearance as follows:

He was painted all down the Breast, between his Shoulders behind; on his Thighs (mostly) before; and the Form of several broad Rings, or Bracelets around his Arms and Legs. I cannot liken the Drawings to any Figure of Animals, or the like; but they were very curious, full of great variety of Lines, Flourishes, Chequered-Work, &c. keeping a very graceful Proportion, and appearing very artificial, even to Wonder, especially that upon and between his Shoulder-blades… I understood that the Painting was done in the same manner, as the Jerusalem Cross is made in Mens Arms, by pricking the Skin, and rubbing in a Pigment.

The crowds came and gawped, and then poor Jeoly succumbed to smallpox, dying in Oxford in 1693. He was not the first, and would not be the last, indigenous Pacific Islander to be dragged back to England as a curiosity. With no natural immunity to Western diseases, they rarely lived to see the benefits of their fame, or of the money brought to their 'benefactors'. In Jeoly's case the lack of respect towards him extended even beyond death: his tattooed skin was removed by surgeons and left hanging on display at the Anatomy School of Oxford University.

It is not known if Defoe visited one of the freakshow booths while Jeoly was alive, but it is highly likely that he would have heard of his fame and been aware of the public interest in such a 'foreign' entity. Did this inspire him to write Man Friday into Crusoe's story? There is no way of knowing, but it could well have been a contributory factor.

One other aspect of Dampier's life may have found its way into Defoe's novel – the way he recounted his thoughts when in the greatest danger. In the course of his career he must have encountered storms galore, but one particular occasion stood out as the most perilous and alarming of all, namely the time he was cast ashore, at his own request, on one of the Nicobar Islands in the Bay of Bengal. It was 1688 and he had been on a privateering expedition raiding shipping in the East Indies. He had with him four natives from the Province of Aceh in modern-day Sumatra, along with an elderly Portuguese sailor and a couple of English crewmen from the ship *Cygnet* on which Dampier had been sailing. Keen to get off the island and head for Aceh, Dampier acquired a canoe from the Nicobar natives. It proved to be far too unstable for a voyage across the open ocean. Dampier lashed poles on either side of the canoe as outriggers, giving a measure of stability. The intrepid voyagers set off and quickly found themselves confronting a violent storm and mountainous seas. Day after day they faced imminent death, with their small craft at the mercy of the elements.

Dampier later wrote of the experience:

The evening of this 18th day was very dismal. The sky looked very black, being covered with dark clouds, the wind blew hard and the seas ran high. The sea was already roaring in a white foam about us; a dark night coming on and no land in sight to shelter us, and our little ark in danger to be swallowed by every wave; and, what was worst of all, none of us thought ourselves prepared for another world. The reader may better guess than I can express the confusion that we were all in. I had been in many imminent dangers before now ... but the worst of them all was but a play-game in comparison with this. I must confess that I was in great conflicts of mind at this time. Other dangers came not upon me with such a leisurely and dreadful solemnity. A sudden skirmish or engagement or so was nothing when one's blood was up and pushed forwards with eager expectations. But here I had a lingering view of approaching death and little or no hopes of escaping it; and I must confess that my courage, which I had hitherto kept up, failed me here; and I made very sad reflections on my former life, and looked back with horror and detestation on actions which before I disliked but now I trembled at the remembrance of. I had long before this repented me of that roving course of life but never with such concern as now. I did also call to mind the many miraculous acts of God's providence towards me in the whole course of my life, of which kind I believe few men have met with the like. For all these I returned thanks in a peculiar manner, and this once more desired God's assistance, and composed my mind as well as I could in the hopes of it, and as the event showed I was not disappointed of my hopes. Submitting ourselves therefore to God's good providence and taking all the care we could to preserve our lives, Mr. Hall and I took turns to steer and the rest took turns to heave out the water, and thus we provided to spend the most doleful night I ever was in. About ten o'clock it began to thunder, lightning, and rain; but the rain was very welcome to us, having drunk up all the water we brought from the island.

These soul-searching reflections, the description of Faith and the simple belief in God's will are entirely in line with the comments made by Defoe in *Robinson Crusoe*, far more so than anything reportedly said by Alexander Selkirk.

As already mentioned in Chapter Three, Dampier was, by a remarkable coincidence, part of the small flotilla which rescued Selkirk in 1709 from his island home during what was Dampier's third and final circumnavigation. Dampier returned to London in 1711 and died there in 1715. His books had brought him fame and a small amount of money but at his death he was substantially in debt. He remains an enigma, a man praised by the poet Coleridge as a genius and 'a man of exquisite mind'. What cannot be denied is his influence on others, and Jonathan Swift is believed to have been inspired by Dampier when he wrote *Gulliver's Travels*. When Captain James Cook set out on his Pacific voyages he carried with him Dampier's charts and books, describing them as 'accurate and authoritative'. Years later, Charles Darwin took a copy of Dampier's collected works with him when he set off on board *Beagle*, revisiting many of the places described by Dampier 150 years earlier.

****

Defoe appears to have been influenced by all of the above stories of shipwreck and survival. He was a journalist, accustomed to drawing on several different sources for the one story. Selkirk may well have prompted Defoe to realise that the underlying tale of hardship and loneliness could sell books. Knox may well have given Defoe the timescale for the story, Pitman may have shown how a well-educated man (as opposed to the rough and ready Selkirk) could plan for survival, and Dampier described the seamanship and experiences of foreign lands. Crusoe is an amalgam, brought together by the magpie-like Defoe, who happily 'borrowed' (or, more accurately in the case of Knox, 'stole') ideas and events described by others.

Part Three

SHIPWRECKED!

Gonzalo, in Shakespeare's The Tempest:

Now would I give a thousand furlongs of sea for an acre of barren ground, long heath, brown furze, any thing. The wills above be done! but I would fain die a dry death.

By Way of Background …

The eighteenth century saw a rapid increase in maritime activity across the globe. The British Navy started to exert its domination around the world – in Europe, off North America and in the Caribbean. This was matched by an explosion in the construction of merchant shipping, reflected in the fact that tonnage went up threefold in the period between 1710 and the end of the century. Hundreds of ships built for the East India Company plied their trade, using the routes around the Cape of Good Hope, across the Indian Ocean, and around the Indian sub-continent. Meanwhile more and more ships were being fitted out for the lucrative slave trade, involving thousands of voyages from England to West Africa, across the Atlantic to the West Indies, and back to England using what became known as the Golden Triangle. Shipping was big business.

Explorers were going further and further in their voyages of discovery – men like William Dampier, Woodes Rogers, Admiral Anson and Captain Cook circumnavigated the globe, spreading the newly charted areas like tentacles around the world. Ships were getting bigger – averaging 700 tons in the 1780s, almost double the average tonnage of a century earlier. The first one-thousand-ton merchant ship was the East Indiaman called *Ceres*, launched in 1787.

With that growth in shipping came a rapid increase in the numbers of sailors employed. By 1800 the population of Britain was around 12 million, of which perhaps 300,000 were seamen of one description or another. Add to that the 33,000 sailors of foreign extraction working on British ships and you realise how vital this sector was to the British economy. It has been estimated that by the time of the Napoleonic Wars roughly one family in six throughout the country was directly dependent upon the sea for their livelihood.

This expansion was matched by an insatiable search for new routes, new ways to cut corners and increase profit margins. This in turn increased the risk of encountering rocks and shallows not marked on the charts of the period. Similarly, the growth in the slave trade in the second half of the eighteenth century meant that more merchants were running the risk of being caught by storms as they entered and left the Caribbean. Nowadays we talk of the 'hurricane season' as being from 1 June to 31 November, although the clear majority of hurricanes are reported in the months of September and October. But there were many reasons why traders were caught out: maybe they were delayed in loading their cargoes at the West African trading stations; maybe the captain was greedy and wanted to get in one more journey before the end of calmer weather; or maybe a rogue hurricane appeared unexpectedly, back in July.

The result could be catastrophic. We live in an era of satellite tracking stations, recording where the eye of the storm is situated, estimating its speed and calculating its point of landfall. We have weather forecasts; we have local radio stations giving hour-by-hour updates. We have evacuation procedures in place, communal shelters, and emergency supplies of water. And even with all these precautions, hurricanes can cause enormous damage, devastating shipping, flattening all structures, and drowning thousands. Consider how much more vulnerable were the colonists living on British plantations in the 1700s, or the sailors trying to seek shelter. If they were close to land they may have had the opportunity, and sense, to drive their vessels into the mangrove swamps to try and ride out the storm. But if they were caught in the open sea, they stood little chance of escape.

Certain years were especially dangerous for shipping. Take the Spanish treasure fleet, prevented from crossing the Atlantic from Mexico to Spain during the duration of the War of the Spanish Succession. The King of Spain had missed his annual consignment of gold and silver bullion for a whole decade and by 1715 he was desperate for funds. He ordered the treasure fleet to sail late in the season, and the eleven ships laden with gold and silver were eleven days out of Cuba when, on 31 July, a storm whipped through the Florida straits and sank the entire fleet with the loss of around 1,000 sailors.

However, one decade stands out as being particularly active for hurricanes: the 1780s. 1780 itself saw a handful of terrible storms, one of which caused the loss of tens of thousands of lives on land. Another, in 1783, caused immense loss of life in the British naval force which had left Jamaica and was heading northwards towards Newfoundland. Together they typify the damage caused by sudden storms, but before looking at them it is worth considering a storm which struck Britain in 1703 – the so-called Great Storm.

Chapter 7

The Great Storm of 1703

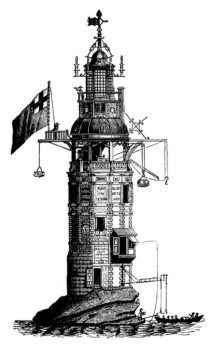

WINSTANLEY'S EDDYSTONE LIGHTHOUSE.

In November 1703 Daniel Defoe tapped the mercury in his wall-mounted barometer and noted with concern that the pressure had plummeted alarmingly. For two weeks strong gale-force winds had lashed the British Isles, quite possibly the remains of a hurricane which had started in the Caribbean and had travelled across the Atlantic, forced on by the prevailing jet stream. Having abated slightly, a new low-pressure system developed rapidly, leading to winds of around ninety miles an hour, with gusts very much higher. As Defoe wrote on 26 November, the mercury 'sunk lower than ever I had observ'd it on any occasion whatsoever, which made me suppose the tube had been handled by the children.'

Meanwhile, thirteen miles south west of Plymouth harbour, on a scattering of rocks in the mouth of the English Channel, a man called Henry Winstanley must have wondered whether he was wise to have issued a statement saying that he wished to be on Eddystone rocks in his lighthouse, 'during the greatest storm there ever was'. His wish was about to come true. His lighthouse, anchored to the rocky base by a dozen heavy iron stanchions, had been alerting shipping to the perils of the area for some five years.

Prior to that, Winstanley had suffered the misfortune of owning two ships which had been destroyed on the unmarked Eddystone rocks. His determination to build a lighthouse led to the impressive feat of erecting a wooden structure, decorated with flags and sporting large wooden candlesticks, in just two years. It is fair to say that Winstanley was no architect and had zero experience of constructing lighthouses, and his splendid contraption featured a fine and richly decorated bed chamber, a stateroom adorned with rich carvings, two closets, a pair of windows, and a kitchen for the use of the men serving as keepers. The task of shipping all the materials out to the site and securing them fully during the couple of hours either side of low tide when access was possible, was no small achievement, spread over a period of two years. That included an interruption when a French privateer destroyed the preliminary work on the footings. Winstanley was carted off to France as a prisoner whereupon Louis XIV ordered his immediate release, saying: 'France is at war with England, not with humanity.' Release enabled Winstanley to go back and finish his lighthouse in November 1698. He was understandably immensely proud of his achievement, as during the subsequent five years not one vessel was wrecked on the notorious hazard to shipping. During that time the lighthouse needed to be strengthened considerably, with granite blocks cladding the timber frame and making it into a twelve-sided structure.

Winstanley had sailed out to the lighthouse to carry out routine maintenance and one imagines that as the winds sharpened and the waves started to scream at the stanchions, Winstanley must have felt a smug satisfaction that his structure could withstand the worst that nature could hurl at it. His confidence was misplaced and by the time the storm subsided twelve days later, there was no trace of the wooden structure, or of any of the stanchions. No sign of Henry Winstanley or of the five workmen who had accompanied him was ever found. Within two days the rocks claimed their first maritime victim for five years, when the cargo ship *Winchelsea*, having crossed the Atlantic laden with a cargo of tobacco, was driven onto the rocks and sank with the loss of all hands on board bar two. When news of the loss of the lighthouse reached London some days after the storm had passed, the Admiralty sent HMS *Lyme* to patrol the waters near the unmarked Eddystone rocks, returning to Plymouth every fourteen days.

What was happening off Plymouth was simply a precursor to what was to occur right across England in what has been described as the worse storm ever to hit the country. In fact, there have been higher winds recorded, but in terms of damage caused it knows no equal. At the time, England was at war with France, and the English Fleet had been assembled off the South Coast, ready to mount an attack on the Spanish city of Cadiz. The English were bottled in, unable to move down the Channel in the face of a strong breeze from the West and had taken refuge off the Kent coast, near the Goodwin Sands. These shallows had traditionally been seen as a good place to shelter and sit out a 'normal' storm, but there was nothing 'normal' about the ferocious gale which unleashed itself over the course of the next few days. Far from offering protection, the Goodwin Sands became a graveyard where Royal Navy ship after ship was driven onto the sandbanks and wrecked.

On shore, roofs across the country were blown off, chimneys crashed down and buildings collapsed. Reports emerged of cattle being lifted off the ground and blown into trees. Queen Anne, who was forced to take shelter in the cellars underneath the palace, described it as 'a Calamity so Dreadful and Astonishing, that the like hath not been Seen or Felt, in the Memory of any Person Living in this Our Kingdom'. It is thought that between 8,000 and 15,000 people lost their lives in the storm. Damage to trade was huge because of the loss of merchant shipping.

The navy was reported at the time to have lost no fewer than thirteen ships, perhaps one fifth of its entire strength in terms of tonnage, along with several thousand sailors. And above all, the storm has remained in the public mind as being one of the worst in history because of one man – Daniel Defoe. The ground-breaking journalist wanted to tell the story of the storm as it unfolded across the country. Nowadays we are used to reporters being sent to venues all over the country, telling their story from the perspective of that particular locality. Before the 1700s this had not been tried – newspaper reports were purely factual accounts, as they filtered through to London (or wherever the paper was being published). Within days of the storm Defoe advertised in the *London Gazette* in the following terms:

> To preserve the Remembrance of the late dreadful Tempest, an exact and faithful Collection is preparing of the most remarkable Disasters which happened on that Occasion, with the Places where, and Persons concern'd, whether at Sea or on Shore.... All Gentlemen that are pleas'd to send any such Accounts, are desired to write no Particulars but what they are satisfied to be true, and to set their Names to the Observations they send, which the Undertakers of this Work promise shall be faithfully Recorded, and the Favour publickly acknowledged.

Those on-the-spot reports, some sixty in number, complete with names, dates and places, enabled Defoe to build up a fascinating story of the storm's progress. The resulting publication of *The Storm, or a collection of the most remarkable Casualties and Disasters which happened in the late dreadful tempest both by sea and land* came to print in 1704. Although it was never a best seller, it made the story of the storm accessible to the public and it has become a yardstick against which all subsequent hurricanes have been measured.

Defoe was not the only person to bring out an account of the Great Storm. In the same year an anonymous publication appeared with its title page carrying the following rather wordy title:

> A wonderful history of all the storms Hurricanes, Earthquakes etc that have happen'd in England for above 500 years past, and the great damages they have done, with a particular and large account of the dreadful storm that happened on the 26th and 27th of November 1703; the loss sustained by sea and land in houses,

churches, people, cattle, corn, hay, trees, shipping and marriners, in England, Flanders and Holland; the natural causes of winds storms earthquakes blazing stars many suns and moons seen at a time dreadful apparitions in the air, fiery dragons and drakes, circles around the sun and moon, rainbows seen in the day and night: An account of the ebbing and flowing of the sea, thunder, lightning, vapours, mists, dews, hail, rain, snow and frost, and lights that lead people out of their way at night, with many other things terrible and amazing. Printed and sold by A Baldwin at the Oxford Arms in Warwick Lane 1704.

Meteorology was still in its infancy back in 1700. Evangelista Torricelli had invented the barometer in 1643, but there was no understanding of how cyclones developed and travelled, no isobar charts, no accurate rain gauges to measure precipitation and no attempt to forecast the weather. The wording to describe wind strengths were woolly to say the least – 'tempest' was used to describe any severe storm, and the idea of grading the wind was not popularised until the introduction of the Beaufort Scale in 1805. Nowadays we are used to hurricanes being categorised from one to four, with One describing a storm with winds of 74 to 95 mph, and Four being reserved for major storms where winds are measured between 130 mph and 156 mph. The Saffir-Simpson Hurricane wind-scale, to give it its proper name, states that with a Category Four hurricane:

Catastrophic damage will occur: Well-built framed homes can sustain severe damage with loss of most of the roof structure and/or some exterior walls. Most trees will be snapped or uprooted and power poles downed. Fallen trees and power poles will isolate residential areas. Power outages will last weeks to possibly months. Most of the area will be uninhabitable for weeks or months.

Contrast this very specific grading with the words available to ship captains who wrote in their logbooks of the weather they encountered that November, using words such as 'grievous storm', 'violent storm', and 'hard gales' before moving on to describe the measures taken on board to try and protect their vessels. Setting aside the hyperbole used at the time to describe the storm, it probably rated no higher than a Category Two under the modern classification.

Even if it is difficult, retrospectively, to measure the severity of the storm which lashed the country, at least Defoe's account gives us a picture of the devastation it caused. Setting aside the damage to land (where the destruction to the coastal ports such as Portsmouth was described by Defoe as 'looking as if the enemy had sack't them and were most miserably torn to pieces'), it is the damage caused to shipping which is of concern here. For several weeks the high winds moving in from the

Atlantic had stopped merchant ships from sailing down the Channel, meaning that merchant and naval shipping alike were hunkered down waiting for the winds to abate. They found no refuge.

The days leading up to the night of 26 November were described by Defoe:

November 24: It had blown exceeding hard, as I have already observed, for about fourteen days past; and that so hard, that we thought it terrible weather: Several stacks of Chimnies were blown down, and several Ships were lost, and Tiles in many Places were blown off from the houses, and the nearer it came to the fatal 26 of November, the Tempestuousness of the weath'r increas'd. On the Wednesday Morning before, being the 24 November, it was fair weather, and blew hard; but not so as to give any Aprehensions, till about 4 o'clock in the Afternoon, the Wind increased, and with Squalls of Rain and terrible Gusts blew very furiously. The collector of these sheets narrowly escap'd the Mischief of a Part of a house, which fell during the Evening of the Day of the Violence of the wind: an abundance of Tiles were blown off the houses that night; the wind continued with Universal violence all the next day and night; and had not the Great Storm followed so soon, this had pass'd for a Great Wind...

The gale moved off to the north-west, but within twenty-four hours had been replaced by the real star of the show, a storm which struck the Welsh coast in the early hours of 27 November before screeching across the width of the country throughout the following twenty-four hours. Defoe recorded: 'about 10 o'clock our barometers informed us that the night would be very tempestuous. The mercury sunk lower than ever I had observed it'. In fact, it is thought that the pressure dropped to around 950 millibars.

In the port of Bristol great damage was caused to the ships in harbour. Flood waters filled the cellars which still run today under the buildings surrounding the city centre, following the medieval street patterns, and the water ruined the extensive stocks of tobacco and sugar being stored there. The anonymous author of *A wonderful history of all the storms ...* states:

At Bristol the storm forced ashore several ships...and some of them were lost particularly the Suffolk and Canterbury store-ships, and the Richard and John lately come from Virginia. This violent storm occasioned so high a tide that many of the warehouses and cellars were overflowed, which damaged great quantities of tobacco, sugar and other goods to a very considerable value viz fifteen thousand pounds and the houses miserably shattered; and a church fell, doing much damage to other buildings.

Laudatur et Alget

Juven. Sat. 1.

Daniel Defoe, from an engraving made in 1706.

Above left: Captain Robert Knox of the East India Company in 1708.

Above right: William Dampier.

An East Indiaman setting sail from the Texel in Holland.

Ships in Distress – English

Shipwrack [sic] – French

Stormy coast scene after a shipwreck.

Ship on fire at night.

Ship wrecked on a rocky coast, 1747.

Storm over a coast.

Above left: Sir Cloudesley Shovell, see chapters 7 & 8.

Above right: English ships at sea.

HMS *Boyne* on fire at Spithead Harbour. See Chapter 11.

Shipwreck off a rocky coast.

Shipwreck, c.1850.

Above left: William Bligh, painted in 1814 when he was a Rear Admiral.

Above right: William Bligh in 1803.

Captain Bligh being forced into the longboat of HMS *Bounty*. See Chapter 16.

All along the south coast, shipping and harbours were damaged, from Falmouth through to Exeter, from Lymington to Portsmouth. The damage to merchant shipping in the Pool of London (just down river from London Bridge) was catastrophic, with Defoe describing literally hundreds of ships breaking their moorings, colliding with each other, and being driven ashore downstream at Limehouse, some two miles away. Many were smashed to pieces as they crashed into each other. In Defoe's words a twisted pile of 700 vessels lay 'in a posture not to be imagined'. Ships lay heaped up on one another, 'the Masts, Boltsprits and Yards split and broke, the Staving Heads and Sterns … the tearing and destruction of rigging … is not to be reckoned.'

Before the storm the Pool of London was full of shipping, ranging from colliers bringing in supplies of coal from Newcastle to ships bringing in sugar from the West Indies and East Indiamen preparing either to leave for the Far East, or waiting to unload cargoes of spices and oriental luxuries. Yet from this melee of ships, just four were left in the Pool the day after the storm had passed, with the rest all swept away. A graphic description of the damage to shipping appears in *A wonderful history of all the storms …*:

> *This storm raged furiously on the Thames breaking a great number of lighters and boats to pieces above Bridge, and a lighter with about an hundred quarters of malt was cast away, as were many others loaden that were driven from the wharfs. It broke the iron chains of some that moored in the open river, shoaled lighters and boats upon the starlings [in other words, the lozenge-shaped structures which protected the columns supporting the bridge] and staved many of them in pieces, so that the surface of the water, the day appearing was seen to be strewd with their wrecks.*

Describing the scene down river from London Bridge the report continues:

> *Between the bridge and Gravesend many Ships and other vessels were driven on shoar and some overset, particularly three East India outward bound ships were driven on shoar and at Blackwall the Sarah Galley had her back broke. A great many lighters and other small vessels and boats were staved or shattered.*

Meanwhile, off the south coast, the naval vessels hoping to ride out the storm were decimated. Throughout the previous century naval ships had been 'rated' according to their size. When Samuel Pepys was appointed Secretary to the Admiralty he amended the classification, linking it less to the number of men carried and more to the number of cannon on board. Under the classification, a first rate ship of the line was described as one which carried between ninety and a hundred guns.

At the other end of the scale a ship rated sixth (i.e. 'a sixth rate') carried between four and eighteen guns. Hoping to ride out the storm off the Goodwin Sands the third rate *Restoration* sank with the loss of 387 lives, including the captain. She had undergone a refit only the previous year and was carrying seventy guns. Her resting place was discovered by divers in the waters off Deal in 1980. The wreck lies just 100 yards or so from another wreck, *Stirling Castle*, also carrying seventy guns. She too had been refitted, in 1699, and was desperately dragging her anchor to try and stop her from running onto the sandbank. She lasted one high-tide longer than *Restoration* before being dragged sideways onto the sandbank, with the loss of all but seventy of the 349 men on board.

In much the same spot another third-rater *Northumberland* succumbed with the probable loss of 253 men. Like the others, she too had undergone a refit, in 1702. The *Mary*, a fourth-rate ship, was wrecked causing the death of 269 men. Whereas the naval ships had names, logbooks and a known number of crew, no such luck was enjoyed by the many merchant ships which may have gathered in the same area off Deal, believing it to be a safe anchorage. Their names may be unknown, but there is no reason to think that they would have been any fewer in number that the Royal Naval vessels. They would have gathered near the Goodwin Sands believing that the area offered shelter from winds originating from both the east and the west. Certainly, the land between Dover and Deal would have been expected to give shelter to the ships anchored off the cliffs below. They would have been waiting for the Thames pilots to guide them out into the Channel, and in great numbers they all succumbed to the ferocity of the storm.

So many ships foundered off Deal that a local shopkeeper by the name of Thomas Powell was reported to be outraged at the lack of public response in the town. Defoe states that the public stood around watching the drama unfold, at best without lending a hand, and at worst waiting for the opportunity for a bit of looting. Powell was so upset that he paid a reward of five shillings for each rescued sailor and commandeered vessels belonging to HM Customs to bring the drowning sailors ashore. Defoe credits him with having rescued 200 sailors, but it is only fair to point out that the good burghers of Deal greatly resented this defamatory account of their inertia and threatened to sue in libel for the damage to their reputation.

Some idea of the chaotic and tragic scenes off Deal are shown in the report of Miles Norcliffe, on board one of the few ships to escape destruction, called *Shrewsberry*:

> *Sir, These Lines I hope in God will find you in good Health, we are all left here in a dismal Condition, expecting every moment to be all drowned: For here is a Great Storm, and is likely to continue; we have here the Rear Admiral of the*

Blew [sic] *in the Ship, call'd the Mary, a third Rate, the very next Ship to ours, sunk, with Admiral Beaumont, and above 500 men drowned; The ship call'd the Northumberland, a third Rate, about 500 Men all sunk and drowned; The Ship call'd the Sterling Castle, a third Rate, all sunk and drowned above 500 Souls; And the Ship call'd the Restoration, a third Rate, all sunk and drowned; These Ships fired their Guns all Night and Day long, poor Souls, for help, but the Storm being so fierce and raging, could have none to save them....There are above 40 Merchant Ships cast away and sunk. To see Admiral Beaumont, that was next to us, and all the rest of his Men, how they climed up the Mast, hundreds at a time crying out for help, and thinking to save their Lives, and in the twinkling of an Eye were drown'd...*

Elsewhere the carnage was repeated – the third-rate *Resolution* off Littlehampton, the sixth-rate *Eagle* and the fifth-rate *Lichfield Prize* off the Sussex coast, the fourth-rate *Newcastle* and the fireship *Vesuvius* off Spithead. *Vanguard*, a second-rate vessel built in Portsmouth in 1678, was caught in Chatham harbour and sank, but without loss of life. One year later she was raised to the surface and was rebuilt in 1710. Remarkably, she remained in use until being broken up in 1769.

Several ships were blown towards the Dutch coast and wrecked, including the fourth-rate *Vigo* and the fifth-rate *Mortar*. It marked the end of a chequered career for *Vigo* – she had originally been launched as *Dartmouth* in 1693, but was captured by the French, then recaptured by the British and renamed in 1702. Rather more fortunate, Admiral Sir Cloudesley Shovell on board *Association* found himself blown from Harwich right across the North Sea as far as Gothenburg in Sweden before he was able to carry out emergency repairs. His ship had been hit by monstrous waves which had filled the upper decks with water, making her highly unstable. Frantic measures were taken to keep *Association* afloat, including cutting down the mainmast and all the rigging, as well as opening hatches so that the water could find its way down to lower levels in the ship where the pumps could operate. The ship nearly ran aground on the sandbanks off the Dutch coast before the winds veered and carried her off towards the coast of Sweden. The admiral was posted 'missing' for a while, and it was two months before his ship was sufficiently repaired to be able to make the return journey.

Two fourth-raters, *Reserve* and *York* went down in Yarmouth and Harwich respectively; 175 men perished on *Reserve* but the captain, the surgeon, the clerk and forty-nine men were saved. Four men lost their lives on *York*.

The extent of the loss must have been devastating to the Navy, especially as it was expected to play a crucial role in the War of the Spanish Succession, which had broken out in 1701 and lasted until 1714. Losing a fifth of its total complement of ships meant a massive period of rebuilding, while the loss of thousands of sailors necessitated a rapid recruitment programme. Suggestions that the navy had lost one third of its workforce are clearly exaggerated but, in the years that followed, the British Navy was to prove less decisive than the army in establishing Britain's upper hand in the conflict. A year prior to the Great Storm an Anglo-Dutch fleet had cornered the Franco-Spanish fleet in the Bay of Vigo and captured a huge amount of gold, silver and treasure. After the storm, the attempt to seize Cadiz was unsuccessful but a year later, in July 1704, the regrouped navy managed to capture Gibraltar.

Her Majesty's Ships *Newcastle*, *Mary*, *Dreadnought*, and *Roebuck* were all launched or rebuilt in 1704, all of them second-raters, while *St Andrew* was to reappear as the first rate *Royal Anne*. The *London*, launched in 1670, underwent a complete rebuild in 1706, but kept her name. In a sense, the timing of the storm could not have been better, since the Navy Board had the whole of the winter to get the fleet back up to strength. Seven second-raters were rebuilt in the period 1704 to 1712, along with thirteen third-raters and seven fourth-raters. This expansion in shipbuilding must have been helped in no small part by the destruction of perhaps 4,000 oak trees which Defoe states had fallen in the New Forest during the Great Storm.

In the aftermath the government declared 19 January 1704 a day of fasting, saying that it 'loudly calls for the deepest and most solemn humiliation of our people'. The storm was generally reckoned by witnesses to represent the wrath of God brought about by the 'crying sins of this nation'. And of course, 'Act of God' lives on as a saying to describe something rare and unpredictable – and generally not covered by insurance.

Chapter 8

The Scillies Storm of 1707

Four years after we last saw Admiral Sir Cloudesley Shovell on board *Association*, heading involuntarily towards Sweden, the revered commander was on his way back from the Mediterranean. Earlier in the War of Spanish Succession he had been involved in the successful seizure of Gibraltar and in the capture of Barcelona. Subsequently, as commander-in-chief of the navy he had led a naval contingent supporting Prince Eugene of Savoy as he lay siege to Toulon and, although the allies failed in their objective, Shovell must have been pleased to be able to extricate his fleet, without serious damage, and to head for home on his flagship before the winter storms set in. It was 22 October 1707 (2 November in the modern calendar) when his flotilla of some twenty-one ships entered the entrance to the English Channel.

The flotilla under Shovell's command included fifteen ships of the line (*Association, Royal Anne, Torbay, St George, Cruizer, Eagle, Lenox, Monmouth, Orford, Panther, Romney, Rye, Somerset, Swiftsure* and *Valeur*) as well as four fireships (*Firebrand,*

Griffin, Phoenix, Vulcan), the sloop *Weazel* and the yacht *Isabella*. There would also have been a miscellany of small transports, tenders and so on.

The area of the Channel was known to have hidden dangers, not least in the area of the Scilly Isles, just off the Cornish Coast. Curiously no one had established exactly where these rocky outcrops lay. At the time, all measurements were taken from the 1697 edition of the '*Seaman's New Kalendar*' by Nathaniel Colson and this, the standard navigation guide of its day, failed to give accurate readings for either latitude or longitude for the Scillies. They were therefore a potential hazard to shipping, which is why a lighthouse had been constructed on the tiny island of St Agnes in 1680. This structure, some 23 metres tall, was topped by a lamp, without a lens. The lamp was originally derived from a coal fire burning in a large open basket called a chauffer and apparently its light could be seen over a great distance – but only if the lighthouse keeper was vigilant in carrying out his duties by riddling the chauffer regularly with a long poker. Writing in around 1750, Robert Heath suggested that this was not always the case:

This light is kept with coals burning near the top of the light-house, which being laid on in large quantities, and sometimes stirred with an iron rod, the ruddy heat and flame are strongly perceived, thro' the glass frames, surrounding it, at a vast distance upon the sea; yet before the coming of this present Light-Keeper, I've known it scarcely perceivable in the night, at the island of St Mary, where it now looks like a Comet. And some are of the opinion, (not without reason) that in the time of the former Light-Keeper it has been suffered to go out, or sometimes not lighted.

The night of 22 October, when Shovell's fleet was approaching the area, was particularly dark and storm-lashed. Earlier that day the admiral had convened a meeting of his fellow captains to reach agreement on their precise position. All but one thought that they were close to Ushant, an area off the coast of Brittany. In fact, they were already some seventy miles north of Ushant, much closer to the Scillies and in particular to the hazardous seas around St Mary's. The lone exception, the captain who correctly identified where they were, was Sir William Jumper on *Lenox*, but not only were his views in the minority, but he was also ordered to detach from the fleet on other duties and therefore was not in a position to reiterate his concerns.

In normal circumstances the lead ships would have been the smaller more manoeuvrable frigates, fifth-raters such as *Phoenix*. But *Phoenix* and the third-rate *Lenox* had both been ordered to go ahead of the others and to make for Falmouth, in order to protect a convoy of merchant ships heading through the Channel. This left the somewhat less agile *Association*, with its much deeper draught, to lead the other ships safely home.

Ship after ship followed *Association* as she headed straight for the rocks, driven by a strong easterly gale. Some warning may have been given by sailors who caught sight of the light from St Agnes, but if so it came too late to avert the tragedy which followed. *Association* was the first to strike, hitting the Outer Gilstone Rock at 8 p.m.; 800 crewmen perished, including the admiral. In vain, cannon shots were fired to alert other shipping. The sinking was described by crewmen aboard *St George*, watching in horror nearby, as having taken place within three or four minutes of the initial impact. *St George* also hit the rocks, suffering considerable damage, but was able to get off thanks to a timely wave which lifted her clear.

Phoenix, which had been ordered to detach itself from the main fleet at around eleven o'clock that morning but was still in the same area, also ran ashore between Tresco and St Martin's, but managed to stay afloat.

Not so lucky was *Eagle*. She struck the appropriately named Tearing Ledge after hitting Crim Rocks. Her exact complement of sailors is not known. Some put it at 234, but there were reports that she was likely to have had around 800 men on board, much the same as on *Association*. All of them perished.

Next up, the fourth-rate *Romney* found itself tangled on Bishop Rock; 289 men perished as the ship was wrecked and slid down to a depth of 130 ft, where she remains to this day. The sole survivor was a man by the name of George Lawrence, a butcher who was found clinging for dear life to a nearby rock.

The fireship *Firebrand* was to meet a similar watery grave, striking the same Outer Gilstone Rock as *Association*. A huge wave lifted her clear and she limped on, badly holed, until she finally came to grief on the southern side of the Western Rocks, near St Agnes. She sank close to the Mengelow Rock, killing twenty-eight of her crew of forty. The surviving officers from *Firebrand* were later called to attend a court martial on board the naval ship *Somerset*, which at that time was having a refit at Blackstakes on the River Medway. The court convened on 21 November 1707 and found that the men were not at fault and that 'both before and after she struck they used the utmost endeavours for saving the ship.'

Alerted by the sound of guns being fired as a warning, some of the ships following in line behind *Association* had lucky escapes. *Royal Anne* narrowly avoided hitting rocks when just a ship's length away from disaster. The rest of the fleet were able to steer away from trouble and headed for home, leaving between 1,500 and 2,000 of their colleagues drowned in the catastrophe. Some reports put the death toll slightly lower, at 1340, but whatever the exact figure it remains one of the greatest peace-time tragedies in the Age of Sail.

For some days afterwards, bodies were being washed ashore. The first account of the tragedy appeared in newspapers the following week, with this report appearing in the *Daily Courant* of 1 November:

[We have] an Account, that Sir Cloudsly Shovel with about 20 Sail of Men of War coming from the Streights, having made an Observation the 21st, lay the 22d from 12 to about 6 in the Afternoon; but the Weather being very hazy and rainy and Night coming on dark, the Wind being S.S.W, they Stearing E by N, supposing they had the Channel open, were some of them upon the Rocks to the Westward of Scilly before they were aware, about 8 a Clock at Night. Of the Association not a Man was sav'd ... The Captain and 24 Men of the Firebrand Fire-Shop were saved, as were also all the Crew of the Phoenix. 'Tis said the Rumney and Eagle, with their Crews, were lost with the Association.

The body of Admiral Shovell was found some seven miles from where his ship went down, immediately alongside the bodies of his dog and his two stepsons, Sir John Narborough and James Narborough. Both were in their early twenties and were the sons of Shovell's wife from her marriage to Rear Admiral Sir John Narborough. Their proximity to each other, and their distance from the wreck site, suggests that they may have managed to get into the ship's longboat but that this capsized and caused them to drown. It was a terrible day for the Narborough family; also drowned was Captain Edmund Loades, the son of Rear Admiral Narborough's sister.

Admiral Shovell was identified by the purser on board *Arundel*, who recognised the body because of the 'black mole under his left ear, also by the joint of one of his fingers being broken inwards. He had likewise a shot in his right arm, another in his left thigh.' The Admiral was buried in the sand on the beach at Porthellick Cove and at a later date a small memorial was erected there. In fact, the admiral's body was later exhumed by order of Queen Anne. Once it had been embalmed in Plymouth, the body was then carried in state to London where it lay on public inspection at the family home in Frith Street, Soho. The body was finally interred in Westminster Abbey at midnight on 22 December 1707, a suitable final resting place for a man regarded as a national hero. Subsequently, an elaborate marble monument designed by Grinling Gibbons was erected in the Abbey. With suitable reverence and little regard for historical accuracy it shows the admiral wearing a large wig and also the costume of a Roman soldier in full armour. The inscription reads:

Sir Cloudesley Shovell Knt. Rear Admirall of Great Britain and Admirall and Commander in Chief of the Fleet. The just rewards of his long and faithful Services. He was deservedly beloved of his Country and Esteem'd tho' dreaded by the Enemy, who had often experienced his Conduct and Courage. Being shipwreckt on the Rocks of Scylly in his voyage from Thoulon. The 22nd of October 1707 at Night in the 57th year of his Age. His fate was lamented by all, But especially the Sea faring part of the Nation to whom he was a Generous Patron and a

*worthy example. His body was flung on the shoar and buried with others in the
sands, but being soon after taken up was plac'd under this Monument which his
Royall Mistress has caus'd to be Erected to commemorate His Steady Loyalty and
Extraordinary Vertues.*

His stepsons were interred in the graveyard at Old Town Church in St Mary's but
with a memorial being put up in the Narborough's family church at Knowlton near
Dover. Other bodies which came ashore in the days and weeks after the wrecks were
buried in mass graves, many of them unmarked.

A number of myths and odd stories developed after the wreck: the first is that a
lad on board *Association* originated from the Scillies, recognised the waters as being
those he had sailed in when at home, and tried to alert the authorities. His reward
for being impudent was (variously) to be disregarded and alternatively to be hanged
from the yardarm for daring to criticise 'those who knew better'. The story first
appeared in the Scilly Isles nearly three quarters of a century after the wreck took
place and is completely without independent evidence.

The second 'myth' concerns the emerald ring which the Admiral habitually wore.
It had been a gift from James Berkeley, at that stage known by the courtesy title of
Viscount Dursley. Learning of the death of her husband and two sons, Elizabeth
Shovell had offered a substantial reward for the return of any items belonging to
the family. Further, she sent Edmund Herbert to Scilly to search for any family
property. In a letter sent in 1709 Herbert indicated that the Admiral's body had first
been found by two women 'stript of his shirt' and specifically commenting on the
fact that 'his ring was also lost off his hand, which however left ye impression on his
finger'. In other words, there was a strong inference that he had been wearing the
ring at the time of death.

There was a subsequent suggestion, some thirty years later, that the two women
had found the Admiral in a half-drowned state, still alive but barely conscious, and
had 'finished him off' in order to steal his ring. Robbing a corpse was one thing,
murdering the drowning man was another; at some stage in the 1730s one of the
women allegedly made a deathbed confession of her crime. Her confidante was a
local clergyman, who allegedly sent the ring back to James Berkeley, by then Third
Earl of Berkeley, and who had been First Lord of the Admiralty in the decade from
1717 to 1727. Quite why the ring was returned to the original donor and not to
the Shovell family is unclear – as is the idea that the dying woman should know
anything at all about the ring's history. Unsubstantiated deathbed confessions make
for a good tale, but there is very little to back up the story. However, there are
reports that an emerald ring matching the description of the original was still in the
Berkeley family in 1879, but no trace of it has since come to light.

The third 'myth' is that the maritime disaster led to such a clamour that Parliament was forced to pass the Longitude Act in 1714. In practice, the navy was much more worried about the state of the compasses in use at the time, rather than blaming the difficulties of establishing longitude. Sir William Jumper on *Lenox*, the man who most accurately assessed the fleet's position, blamed his compass for various navigational errors and his comments prompted the navy to order an examination of all the compasses on board the ships which survived the ordeal, as well as on ships in harbour at Portsmouth. These boxed compasses were generally made of inferior metal, which corroded and caused faulty readings and it must have dismayed the Navy Board to find that only nine of the 112 compasses which they tested were accurate and in a serviceable state.

Other factors at the time focused on the inaccuracies in the charts made available to sailors, and to the fact that measurements were often given from different points, according to whichever navigation manual was being used. Later research also shows human error – failure to follow normal procedures, leading to faulty readings. The one thing which was not suggested at the time was that the losses were attributable to the fact that none of the ships knew their exact longitude. They were just as ignorant of their latitude.

It is therefore more accurate to say that what prompted the passing of the Longitude Act in 1714 was not public clamour for a solution, linked to the tragic loss of Shovell's fleet, but to the lobbying of the mathematicians William Whiston and Humphrey Ditton. In June 1714 they published a pamphlet entitled 'Reasons for a Bill, Proposing A Reward for the Discovery of the Longitude'. They listed eleven reasons for the Bill before Parliament, with item ten being that, 'It will prevent the Loss of abundance of Ships and Lives of Men; as it would certainly have sav'd all Sir Cloudsly Shovel's Fleet, had it been then put in practice'.

Three of the eleven reasons propounded by Whiston and Ditton were linked to their idea for a series of signal ships along the English Channel. Central to this idea was a plan to shoot rockets from a row of static ships, in known positions, so that vessels in the area could establish longitude by measuring how long it took sound and light to reach them – much as with thunder and lightning. Whitson was however a figure of fun, not least because of his various eccentricities, and he was often satirised and mocked by his contemporaries.

In July 1714, a month after the initial pamphlet, Whiston and Ditton published a full description of their scheme under the title of *A New Method for Discovering the Longitude both at Sea and Land*. No mention was made of the Scillies tragedy and what comes across is that Whiston in particular was keen to see the establishment of the Longitude Board, and the setting up of a prize fund, so that he could eventually claim the reward himself.

The result of all this pressure on Parliament was that on 9 July 1714, Queen Anne gave her royal assent to an 'Act for Providing a Publick Reward for such Person or Persons as Shall Discover the Longitude at Sea'. The value of the reward of £20,000 would be worth close to £2 million today.

Over the years Whiston submitted repeated claims to the Board but was on each occasion turned down. His plan for using magnetic variations was submitted in 1719, and for measuring solar eclipses in 1724. In 1730 he proposed a scheme using eclipses of Jupiter's satellites. These were first discovered in 1610 by Galileo Galilei with the use of the new-fangled telescope. They provided what was, in effect, a celestial timepiece which was visible at the same time from different points on Earth.

Other mathematicians came up with their own tables based upon astronomical observations. In particular Nevil Maskelyne produced pre-computed lists showing the future position of the moon. These were available from 1768 onwards under the title *Nautical Almanac and Astronomical Ephemeris* and set out tables for each following year. Meanwhile, back in 1754, James Bradley had commissioned the London instrument maker John Bird to make a brass instrument which, during sea trials, was to become the world's first marine sextant, accurate for measuring longitude within a single degree. Developed out of the more limited octant of the early 1750s, the sextant quickly proved popular and was used by James Cook in the third of his voyages to the Pacific. It had been based upon the ideas of the German mathematician Tobias Mayer who had come up with a method of measuring lunar distance using a repeating circle. It earned Mayer an award of £3,000 from the Longitude Board.

Much is made nowadays of the efforts made by John Harrison in coming up with a marine chronometer capable of recording time accurately over the course of the months and even the years of an ocean voyage, notwithstanding changes in temperature, pressure and so on, and despite the rolling motion of the sea. This was central to the ability to measure astronomical features by reference to a known, fixed point in time, in order to arrive at a measurement of longitude. However, it has to be said that Harrison's invention had very little impact on shipping during the eighteenth century. He came up with his revolutionary clock 'H4' in 1761 and it was tested in 1765 and, as is well known, he was awarded £10,000 by the Longitude Board, albeit somewhat begrudgingly. He was also given a further payment of £8,750 in 1773, by which time Harrison was nearly 80 years old.

The fact remains that in the eighteenth century navigation was much more likely to have been based on locating longitude by reading charts linked to the position of our moon, and of the moons of Jupiter, than it was upon any chronometer based on Harrison's design. It was not until 1825 that the navy routinely equipped its ships with marine chronometers.

Chapter 9

The Loss of HMS *Victory* in 1744

When the news of what had happened on the night of 5 October 1744 became known, the British public were aghast. How could it happen? How could the largest ship in the British Navy simply disappear? The ship, the *Victory*, was the nation's pride and joy, a monster of a fighting machine which demonstrated, time and time again, the superiority of its firepower over its French counterparts. So how could she disappear, in the English Channel so close to home, when other ships in the same area reached safety as a gale passed through? In modern parlance, it had been blowing a hooley, but nothing life-threatening. And yet *Victory*, with a gun deck 174 ft long and carrying no fewer than 110 cannon, disappeared in the storm. What made it all the more strange was that no one really knew exactly where the disappearance took place. It was thought to be somewhere near Alderney in the Channel Islands. People thought that they had heard guns being fired as a distress signal, and the finger of suspicion pointed at the keeper of the lighthouse built on Casquets Rocks – had he failed to keep the fires burning? Had he failed to warn *Victory* of its approach to what had been called 'the graveyard of English shipping'?

In the days and weeks after the mighty ship disappeared, wreckage started to be washed up on a number of the Channel Islands; Alderney, Guernsey and Jersey included. But no trace whatsoever was found of the 1,150 men on board who were lost, presumed drowned.

The ship had been launched in Portsmouth Dockyard just seven years earlier, built to the designs of master shipwright Joseph Allin. Like Allin, many of the crew came from Portsmouth. Construction had taken nearly ten years, a decade which saw constant arguments between the Admiralty and the ship builder. The Navy wanted something low-slung and stable: Allin wanted something magnificent, high and roomy. Each of her three main gundecks carried twenty-eight brass cannon. In addition, she carried a dozen six-pound guns on her quarter deck and another four on the forecastle. And those guns were rather special, because they were all made of brass. So special that they had been commissioned before the ship herself had been ordered. She was the last warship in Britain to have brass cannon – afterwards, cheaper iron cannon were preferred. Some of the guns were massive, forty-two pounders capable of devastating enemy shipping. But her design made her top-heavy, particularly with all those guns, some of which would have weighed as much as four tons. Even during her sea trials important changes had to be made to increase her stability. Basically, she was too high out of the water and too long for her width, meaning that with a following wind she had a tendency to be pushed downwind and onto the shore. Her lack of stability was to prove fatal.

She was originally used as the flagship for Sir John Norris, in charge of the Channel Fleet, but in July 1744 as the War of Austrian Succession proceeded she was called upon to head for Portugal to rescue a Mediterranean convoy of British ships which had been boxed in on the River Tagus. If the Brest fleet succeeded in forcing the blockaded ships to surrender, Britain risked losing the entire war. Cometh the hour cometh the man, and that meant bringing Admiral Balchin, then aged 74, out of retirement. Here was a man with fifty-eight years' service to king and country, a man who had served on thirteen different warships, and who had risen to become Admiral of the White, the second highest office in the entire navy. He was a brilliant commander, much loved by the men who served under him and one imagines that he was proud to give up his retirement job, as governor of the Royal Hospital for Seamen at Greenwich, to sail once more on active service.

He used *Victory* as his flagship, sailed to Portugal with a convoy of around thirty ships, liberated the convoy and then chased the retreating French navy down to Cadiz. It all marked a magnificent finale to an illustrious naval career, but for Admiral Balchin there was to be no hero's return. As *Victory* entered the Channel and approached the Channel Islands she lost sight of the rest of the fleet. She was last seen as the light began to fade on the afternoon of 4 October, wallowing in the swell as a gale started to build. More recent calculations suggest that, as she tilted, she took on board a massive amount of water through her open galleries, washing perhaps 3 metres of water down into the hold. Such a body of water, rushing from side to side in an already unstable vessel, would have made *Victory* lurch violently from side to side, eventually causing her to topple over. She disappeared along with all on board. Later, much was made of the fact that in addition to her normal crew she had around fifty volunteers drawn, it was said, from the most noble families in the country.

The navy needed a scapegoat, and so immediately set about court-martialling the Casquets Lighthouse keeper. The lighthouse actually consisted of three towers, constructed in 1724, each burning a fire in a lantern. The configuration resulted in a horizontal triangle of lights, easily distinguishable from other lights in the area. The three lights were called *St Peter, St Thomas* and *Dungeon* and were first used on 30 October 1724. One of the towers, since extended, is still in use today as part of the fully automated network of lighthouses controlled by Trinity House. Back in 1744 Trinity House had leased the towers to Thomas Le Cocq, who owned the jagged rocks and who paid a licence fee of £50 per annum for the right to operate the lights. In return he was given the right to charge a fee of a halfpenny per ton to each passing ship and it has been calculated that by 1744 this was producing an annual income of around £650. The patent granted to Le Cocq specifically required him to keep the lights constantly burning in 'ye night season whereby seafaring men and mariners might take notice and avoid ye dangers.' His income would have dropped in the years when Britain was at war with France, because commercial trade diminished, but it still remained a profitable venture and there is no reason to believe that he failed in his duty to 'keep the home fires burning'.

In any event, Le Cocq was in no way to blame: *Victory* went down nowhere near the Casquets. He was only exonerated when the wreck was finally pinpointed over two and a half centuries later, over sixty nautical miles away (110 kilometres) in May 2008. What then was the real cause of the disappearance? In part the faulty design, already mentioned, may have been a contributing factor, but the other significant problem was her actual construction. *Victory* was a ship old before her time; old because she never was an entirely new ship when she was built in Portsmouth just ten years earlier. The decision was made to build her using timbers from a much older ship, an earlier *Victory* which had caught fire in 1721 while works known as 'breaming' were carried out to burn off weed and marine growth from the underside of her hull. Rather than start from scratch, it was decided to reuse these older timbers, some dating back to the launch of the earlier *Victory* in 1675. At that stage she had been known as *Royal James* but had been renamed *Victory* in 1691. After the fire she was broken up and the usable timbers set aside for future use. Management of timbers in the dockyard appears to have been chaotic, with old seasoned wood stored alongside planks cut from unseasoned timber. The carpenters working on the unseasoned wood must have known that the wood was not right for the job, but perhaps they knew what the naval authorities already knew, that this short-sightedness was going to lead to extra work down the line. Up until the 1720s the average life of a Royal Navy ship, before she needed to have a refit, was anything up to seventeen years. By 1740 this had halved. The reason: a shortage of suitable timbers.

The causes were historic – the rebuilding of the City of London, after the Great Fire in 1666, consumed large stocks of timber. The Anglo-Dutch Wars meant that many ships were lost and needed to be replaced. Timber was being cut down and not replaced with younger plantations of oak trees. The Great Storm of 1703 would have brought down a great many trees, at a time when there was a massive period of shipbuilding. All these factors together meant that there simply was not a decent stock of slow-grown oak with which to build the ships. Instead, the navy resorted to using newer, faster growing oak. In the forty years leading up to the construction of *Victory* the winter seasons had been remarkably warm and wet, causing a growth-spurt in trees, but also ensuring that the wood was full of sap. This simply would not dry out and any attempt at seasoning the wood failed because it would rot before it dried. Worse, by storing this wet unseasoned wood alongside older seasoned timbers in poorly ventilated areas, the dockyard simply created the conditions where wet and dry rot could spread.

Victory was therefore a typically shoddy piece of early to mid-eighteenth-century workmanship. She looked good, she packed a huge punch, but she was not very seaworthy and she was in a poor state of repair. The navy may have blamed the magnitude of the storm for the loss but, in reality, the blame lay squarely at their door. After all, that would explain why all the other ships in Balchen's convoy got home safely.

None of this explains why an American company called Odyssey Marine Exploration started to take an interest in locating the wreck of *Victory*. Odyssey, originally founded in 1994 as Remarc International and registered in Tampa, Florida, has in the past used publicity material confirming that Odyssey is a treasure-seeking enterprise (as opposed to an archaeological specialist). The company is understood to be interested in bringing up the brass cannon, as well as an alleged fortune in gold bullion. Having located the wreck in 2008, the company entered into an agreement with the British Government, but it is unclear whether the terms of that agreement have been adhered to and the Ministry of Defence has since carried out its own independent assessment of the state of the wreck. *Victory* was, after all, a Royal Navy warship belonging to the Ministry of Defence, but ownership of the site has now been transferred to a charitable organization called the Maritime Heritage Foundation.

A decision was made to allow further exploration and the removal of artefacts, based on the threat of increased damage to the site as a result of the activities of deep-sea trawlers in the area, and of natural erosion. However, the motives of the people behind the project have been called into question and, faced with a threat of judicial review, this consent was then suspended. Already, at least one brass cannon has been brought up by a rogue Dutch salvor working in the area. The find was seized by Dutch customs officials when it was revealed during a search for drugs and contraband.

It is highly unlikely that it will be possible to raise the wreck, but presumably some further work will be allowed. The question of 'who gets to keep any treasure' has yet to be resolved and indeed the whole project, involving a partnership with a treasure-seeking company, is thought to be contrary to UNESCO's insistence that the profit motive should not be paramount. The UNESCO Convention on the Protection of the Underwater Cultural Heritage states that the preservation of a wreck *in situ* has to be the starting point. The terms of the agreement entered into between the British Government and Odyssey relating to any treasure which might be recovered has not been fully disclosed. In theory, eighty per cent of the value of any gold bullion recovered from the wreck could pass to Odyssey Marine Exploration, subject to approval by the Receiver of Wrecks. Small wonder that the arrangement has been challenged in the House of Lords, where parliamentary privilege has meant that opponents of the scheme have been able to throw around words such as 'scam' to describe the arrangements, both with Odyssey and with The Maritime Heritage Foundation. Questions have also been raised about the independence of the Foundation, based on the overlap in personnel between the two groups.

So, where did the story of buried treasure come from? Even as early as 23 October 1744, just days after *Victory* went missing, the *Amsterdamsche Courant* carried an article expressing concern at the lack of information about *Victory*, saying that the uncertainty had pushed up premiums for insurable items on board *Victory* by fifteen per cent. Royal Navy ships were not insured and this can only have referred to insurance of non-Government property on board – such as bullion and other freight. A week later, the same paper carried the story of the loss with the words: 'People will have it that on board of the *Victory* was a sum of 400,000 pounds sterling that it had brought from Lisbon for our merchants.'

Such a volume of gold, presumably in the form of single, double and quadruple moidores, would have weighed around four tons. Moidores were regularly in use in London by merchants of all nationalities and quite possibly were even more commonly seen in circulation than the English equivalent, i.e. the guinea, and its smaller fractions.

Is such a report credible? Yes, certainly, because Lisbon was the bullion capital of Europe at the time and during the blockade the country had been unable to ship its gold to Britain and Northern Europe. In peacetime the shipments would have typically been made by boats operating out of Falmouth, yet obviously the bullion houses in Lisbon would have been delighted that there was a ship of the size and invincibility of *Victory* to act as courier immediately after the blockade had been lifted.

Such cargoes being carried 'on the side' by naval ships was apparently not without precedent, as borne out by the detailed study of records contained in Sean Kingsley's book *'Oceans Odyssey: Deep-Sea Shipwrecks...'*. The author, Dr Kingsley of Wreck Watch International, is a well-respected marine archaeologist with many years' experience. He is quite open about the fact that he is also archaeological consultant to both Odyssey and MHF. On the other hand, a report by Wessex Archaeology, commissioned by English Heritage on behalf of the Department for Culture, Media and Sport, found no evidence of any government bullion shipment at the time and therefore concluded that no significant quantity of valuable bullion or prize cargo was likely to be present at the wreck site.

It is also worth mentioning that it was 'common knowledge' that while Admiral Balchin was in Portugal he had captured a number of vessels trading out of Martinique in the West Indies. If so, he can reasonably have been expected to have been carrying back the proceeds of sale of any goods captured, if not the goods themselves, on board *Victory*.

The debate has to be seen in context of the fact that only a commercial operation, backed by private funding and therefore expecting a return on its investment, could possibly afford to undertake the exploration of the site, which lies beyond the depth at which divers can freely operate. A submersible would be needed, and a submersible costs money.

All this speculation does not prove that *Victory* was a treasure ship, but it certainly explains why Odyssey and the Maritime Heritage Foundation were particularly keen to start work on examining the wreck site and bringing artefacts to the surface. This is obviously an aspect of the story which will run and run, but in the meantime the loss of *Victory* remains as a huge human tragedy. To put it in perspective, 1,503 lives were lost on Titanic. *Victory* lost 1,150, or thereabouts, not in some distant seas 400 miles off Newfoundland, but less than 100 miles out of Plymouth harbour. It can only be hoped that the final resting place of such a large number of naval personnel is fully respected and preserved, which is perhaps why the direct descendants of Admiral Balchin, via his daughter, are adamant that they wish to see the site left undisturbed.

Chapter 10

The Hurricanes of 1780 and 1782

1780 in the Caribbean meant that Britain was five years into the American Revolutionary War – although in practice, it was seen more as a general war of attrition between Great Britain and France, both of whom were constantly seeking to gain the ascendancy in a power struggle right across the Caribbean. Of particular significance, 1780 was marked by a series of hurricanes. These caused immense damage to the islands and wrecked a great number of both French and British naval vessels. They caused the deaths of an estimated 22,000 men, women and children, and presaged a downturn in island economies throughout the Caribbean. Famine and death by starvation followed in the wake of the storms, with the slave communities being especially hard hit.

It had started back in June – very early in the hurricane season – when the San Antonio hurricane swept through St Lucia, causing 4–5,000 deaths. It had then moved on to Puerto Rico, before passing over what is now the Dominican Republic, leaving a swathe of destruction in its path. August saw a violent storm hit St Kitts, causing widespread damage to crops. But these were small beer compared to the Savanna La Mar hurricane which developed in the Southern Caribbean on 1 October.

Among the first casualties was the British transport ship *Monarch*, which sank with the loss of its entire crew, along with several hundred Spanish prisoners. The storm headed for Jamaica, hitting landfall at the port of Savanna-la-Mar on 3 October. The islanders had gathered to watch the spectacle when a tidal surge swept through, drowning hundreds, swamping ships and virtually destroying the entire town; 400 people were drowned in the port of Lucea, with much the same number perishing at Montego Bay. The British frigate *Phoenix* lay in the path of the storm; it sank with the loss of its two hundred crew. A similar fate was visited on three ships-of-the-line, *Victor*, *Scarborough* and *Barbadoes*. Dozens of other ships were lost (including *Deal Castle* and *Endeavour*) or were severely damaged, including seven which were dismasted. *Stirling Castle*, a third rater, was destroyed off the coast of Cuba on 5 October with the loss of nearly all on board. The storm then tailed off towards Cuba and the Bahamas and, in all, fatalities were numbered at around 3,000.

But all that paled into insignificance compared with the storm which brewed up a few days later. In all probability it had started off the Cape Verde Islands, as most Caribbean hurricanes do, picking up strength as it crossed the Atlantic. By the time it had finished its path of destruction it had caused incalculable damage and destroyed entire economies in the region, earning its name of The Great Hurricane.

The first place to be hit was Barbados, late on 10 October. In his report on the storm the island's governor Major General Cunninghame wrote:

> *The armory was leveled to the ground, and the arms scattered about. The buildings were all demolished; for so violent was the storm here, when assisted by the sea, that a 12 pounder gun was carried from the south to the north battery, a distance of 140 yards. The loss to this country is immense: many years will be required to retrieve it.*

To lift a cannon capable of firing a twelve-pound ball speaks volumes for the destructive power of the gusts.

Some fifty years after the Great Hurricane had passed, the editor of a Barbadian paper entitled *The West Indian* mentioned the violence of the storm with the words:

> *At dawn of day (October 10th), the wind [came] rushing with a mighty force from the northwest. Towards evening the storm increased, and at nine o'clock had attained its height, but it continued to rage till four next morning, when there was*

a temporary lull. Before day-break, the castle and forts, the church, every public building and almost every house in Bridgetown, were leveled with the earth.

Writing to his wife a month after the storm, Admiral Sir George Brydges Rodney was moved to say this about the storm on Barbados:

The strongest buildings and the whole of the houses, most of which were stone, and remarkable for their solidity, gave way to the fury of the wind, and were torn up to their foundations; all the forts destroyed, and many of the heavy cannon carried upwards of a hundred feet from the forts. Had I not been an eyewitness, nothing could have induced me to have believed it. More than six thousand persons perished, and all the inhabitants are entirely ruined.

Another contemporary indication of the violence of the storm on Barbados is shown in a letter from Dr Gilbert Blane to a Dr Hunter in which he writes: 'what will give as strong an idea of the force of the wind as anything, many of them [the trees] were stripped of their bark.'

If this is accurate, it must have entailed a wind gusting in excess of 200 mph, because experiments have shown that nothing less than a wind-speed of that magnitude would strip bark.

A later book by the French geographer Reclus, written in 1873, stated: 'Starting from Barbados, where neither trees nor dwellings were left standing, it caused the English fleet anchored off St. Lucia to disappear and completely ravaged this island, where 6000 persons were crushed under the ruins.'

St Lucia suffered dreadfully with Castries, the main town and port, almost flattened. In particular all the barracks and huts for His Majesty's troops and all official buildings on the island were blown down, and it was said that there were only two houses left standing in the town.

Another report mentioned that one of the ships in harbour was driven ashore with such force that it landed on top of the roof of the building used as a hospital – and flattened it. Poor Admiral Rodney: his entire fleet in Castries Harbour was destroyed, either in the gales or in the tidal surge which followed. Other European countries incurred similar losses, with the Dutch losing eleven ships, fully laden with produce ready to be carried back to Holland, off the coast of Grenada. Another eight Dutch ships were also destroyed elsewhere. Reclus continues his account:

After this, the whirlwind tending toward Martinique, enveloped a convoy of French transports, and sunk more than 40 ships carrying 4000 soldiers; on land,

the town of St. Pierre and other places were completely razed by the ground, and
9000 persons perished there.

In fact, it has been estimated that 1,000 people died in St Pierre alone, and of course most of the loss of life would not have been in the big stone houses, built with sturdy cellars, but in the shacks and slave quarters.

By now it was 11 October. The forward speed of the hurricane has been estimated at a slow six nautical miles an hour, but the winds within the storm continued to gust in excess of 150 mph. It meant that the storm took a long time to pass through. The editor continues:

More to the north, Dominique, St Eustatius, St Vincent and Porto Rico were
likewise devastated and most of the vessels which were on the path of the cyclone
foundered, with all their crews. Beyond Porto Rico, the tempest bent to the north-
east, toward the Bermudas and though its violence had gradually diminished, it
sunk several English warships returning to Europe.

The death toll in St Eustatius has been put at 4,500. The path of destruction reached Santo Domingo (the present day Dominican Republic) on 14 October, where much coastal damage was caused by the 6-metre surge which followed the storm. It then reached Bermuda four days later, where it is estimated that fifty ships were destroyed off the coast. The last effects of the storm were noted off Newfoundland on 20 October, south-east of Cape Race.

There is no doubting that the hurricane left the English navy in a substantially weaker state in the aftermath of the storm: among the ships which Admiral Rodney lost were *Phoenix* and *Blanche*. Two smaller naval frigates, *Andromeda* and *Laurel* were wrecked off Martinique. However, some of the worst losses occurred to the British fleet under the command of Vice Admiral Peter Parker. He was based in Port Royal, Jamaica and lost the 72-gun third-rate ship of the line *Thunderer*. Among the crew killed on board was the second child of Captain James Cook (midshipman Nathaniel Cook, aged 16).

Astonishingly, the Great Hurricane was followed almost immediately by another one, known as Solano's Hurricane. For many years it was assumed that this was in fact the same storm and it was first noticed on 15 October, off the coast of Jamaica. On October 20, 1780 the storm had reached hurricane force and struck the Spanish fleet under the command of Admiral Don José Solano y Bote Carrasco y Díaz. His sixty-four ships were transporting 4,000 troops, led by Field Marshal Don Bernardo de Gálvez y Madrid, from Havana, Cuba. Their mission was to carry out an attack on British-held Pensacola in West Florida, but the storm caused so much damage to the fleet that the attack was cancelled. Half of the invasion force was drowned and it was to be May the following year before Gálvez was able to mount another attack.

What then of the effect of the 1780 hurricane season? The Caribbean islands had been enjoying a decade of comparative prosperity but this ended with a sudden jolt. It is estimated that on Barbados it took four years for sugar production to recover. All the sugar mills had been destroyed and had to be rebuilt. Not a single plantation on the island was left undamaged, and many plantation owners simply abandoned their land and returned to Britain. On St Lucia, within four years of the Great Hurricane there were an estimated 300 abandoned plantations and as a result several thousand abandoned slaves had disappeared into the interior. Throughout the Caribbean there were food shortages and deaths attributable to starvation, especially among the slaves.

On the naval front, both France and Britain operated with reduced fleets. Britain had planned to launch an attack on Puerto Rico, which would have greatly increased British influence and power in the region, but this had to be abandoned. Overall, Britain lost about the same number of servicemen to the effects of the hurricane in just seven days as were killed in battle in the entire War of American Independence.

It would of course be overstating matters to suggest that the naval losses contributed greatly to the outcome of the war, but the lessening of British influence in the Caribbean, and the feeling that 'it was all too expensive to keep a naval presence in the area', and 'is it really worth it?' may have helped persuade Britain to throw in the towel.

***

If the Great Hurricane of 1780 was the greatest killer storm in the Northern Hemisphere of all time, the storm which engulfed the British fleet just two years later resulted in the greatest loss of sailors in a single incident. Some 3,500 men perished in a single storm, which became known as the Central Atlantic Hurricane of 1782.

Towards the end of July 1782 Admiral Graves had left the port of Bluefields on the south west of Jamaica, bound for England. He had with him a number of French ships captured in the Battle of the Saintes in April 1782. That battle had been an important British victory, not least because it averted an invasion of Jamaica by the French forces. But it was also a battle where it seemed that the British Navy managed to 'snatch defeat from the jaws of victory' in the sense that they failed to press home their advantage and a number of French vessels escaped.

The French second-rate *Gloriuex* sank under a fierce bombardment and *César* was dismasted and then captured by the British *Centaur*. The following night a fire broke out on *César*, resulting in the loss of the ship along with 400 French sailors. Also killed were fifty British sailors who were aboard, having taken her as a prize of war.

The French commander Comte de Grasse was captured at the Battle of the Saintes, along with his flagship, the 120 gun *Ville de Paris*. In that battle around 3,000 French sailors had lost their lives and some 5,000 soldiers and sailors had been taken prisoner. The British force under Admiral George Rodney lost around 250 men, but succeeded in capturing the 74-gun ship *Hector* and the 64-gun *Ardent*. Shortly after the main battle Sir Samuel Hood captured the 74-gun gun *Caton* at what was termed the Battle of the Mona Passage.

These captured vessels, many of them barely seaworthy and severely undermanned, all accompanied Admiral Graves, on board *Ramillies*, when he set off for England. He had with him *Ardent*, *Centaur* and *Pallas* together with a number of British merchant ships, when they set sail to cross the Atlantic. A month into the voyage *Ardent* was forced to return to Jamaica for repairs, unable to continue with the Atlantic crossing. On 8 September *Caton* developed a bad leak and decided to head for Halifax, Nova Scotia, accompanied by *Pallas* as an escort. *Caton* was eventually refitted but only ever served as a hospital ship. *Pallas* limped across the Atlantic but sprang a leak off the Azores and was eventually destroyed by fire in February 1783.

On 17 September 1782 the main squadron was struck by a violent storm off the banks of Newfoundland. Winds of 150 mph accompanied a ferocious thunderstorm. Huge waves were whipped up, catching the ships off balance. Depleted crews frantically tried to operate the pumps, but ship after ship lost main and mizzen masts. Rudders snapped and numerous ships began to sink as timbers split and opened up under the tremendous pressure of the waves. Of the other warships only *Canada* and *Jason* reached England. *Ramillies* was so badly damaged that she was abandoned and then set on fire by the captain, who was the last man on board. This was only after the frantic officers and crew had spent three days, round the clock, trying to pump out the water which was gushing in through her split sides. Some years later the marine artist Robert Dodd painted a series of four paintings showing the final hours of *Ramillies*: 'A storm coming on', 'The Storm increas'd', 'The Ramillies Water Logg'd with her Admiral & Crew quitting the Wreck', and 'The Ramillies Destroyed'. These were then brought out as a series of coloured mezzotints some twelve years after the events shown.

A report of the time stated that the cabin where the Admiral lay on board *Ramillies* was flooded and that his cot-bed was,

> *jerked down by the violence of the shock and the ship's instantaneous revulsion, so that he was obliged to pull on his boots half leg deep in water, to huddle on wet clothes, and get on deck. At dawn of day, the people of the Ramillies beheld the Dutton, formerly an East India-man, go down head foremost, the fly of her ensign being the last thing visible.*

The report went on to say that 'of the ninety-four or ninety-five sail seen the day before, hardly twenty could now be counted'.

The captured French vessels *Ville de Paris*, *Glorieux* and *Hector* all sank in the storm. In the case of *Ville de Paris* all but one of the 800 men on board drowned. Another ship which foundered and sank was the British ship *Centaur*. She had originally been captured from the French some twenty years earlier and was now under the command of Captain Inglefield. Remarkably, the captain and eleven of his men survived and managed to get into one of the ship's pinnaces. In a later 'Narrative', published in 1783, he describes their predicament with the words:

> *We were altogether twelve in number, in a leaky boat, with one of the gunwhales stove, in nearly the Middle of the Western Ocean, without compass, without quadrant, without sail, without great coat or cloak, all very thinly cloathed, in a gale of wind, with a great sea running!*

For sixteen days they survived at sea with only two quart bottles of fresh water between them. They did however have a minute amount of spoilt bread and some ship's biscuits, along with a piece of pork and a small ham. A blanket was found at the bottom of the pinnace, and was 'bent between one of the stretchers and under it we scudded all night, in expectation of being swallowed up by every wave…'

They managed to catch rain as it fell into containers such as the implement used for baling, securing an extra six quarts. Each daybreak a single biscuit was broken into twelve pieces and shared out equally, and the same happened for supper. After a fortnight the men were in a terrible condition, suffering all over from body sores and from the effects of starvation.

One man, the quarter-master Thomas Matthew, died on the fifteenth day at sea. It made for a particularly sombre evening meal. Up until then, Inglefield had got each man to sing a song or tell a story, but that night there was no singing and no storytelling, just an enveloping silence as each man contemplated his fate.

On the sixteenth day the men saw rolling fog banks, which gave the appearance of there being land on the horizon, but later in the day their disappointment turned to euphoria when they realised that the fog was hanging over land, namely the island of Faial in the Azores. Their arrival after such an appalling journey was considered miraculous, but not so fortunate were the 600 other crew who were drowned on board *Centaur*.

Captain Inglefield returned to Britain and, as was standard in all such cases, had to face a court martial to ascertain whether he was responsible for the loss of *Centaur*. The hearing was on 25 January 1783. After hearing the evidence of his 'great and manly exertions' and his 'cool and resolute conduct', he was acquitted of all blame. He remained in the navy and actually sat as one of the judges on the Court Martial of the men accused of mutiny involving HMS *Bounty* (see Chapter Sixteen).

Getting back to the scene of destruction off Newfoundland: of the merchant ships, *Dutton*, *British Queen*, *Withywood*, *Rodney*, *Ann*, *Minerva* and *Mentor* all foundered. Admiral Graves had been forced to transfer from *Ramilles* on to the merchant ship *Belle* and on board that vessel finally reached Cork in Ireland on 10 October. The storm had proved to be one of the worst disasters ever to befall the Royal Navy and the autumn of 1782 was a particularly painful one for the Admiralty, since it had lost *Royal George* less than one month earlier (see next chapter).

Chapter 11

Human Error: Fire and Water

Sinking of HMS *Royal George* at Spithead, 29 August 1782.

The Royal Navy records of ships which were lost in the Georgian era (excepting those which were destroyed as a result of enemy action) contain various causes for the loss: there were many incidents where ships had been sunk after striking hidden rocks; there were others where faulty charts or faulty navigation had been involved; and many where adverse weather conditions had caused a ship to capsize, or lose a mast or rudder and hence become impossible to control. But there were also a number of cases involving negligence, sometimes in very public and humiliating circumstances and none were more embarrassing than the loss of *Royal George* in 1782.

Ordered to be constructed back in August 1746 and finally launched in February 1756, she was a giant of a ship, the largest in the world. A first-rate ship of the line, she saw illustrious action during the Seven Years War particularly at the Battle of Quiberon Bay in 1759. In 1780 she took part in the Battle of Cape St Vincent. Her massive arsenal of 100 guns, which included twenty-eight forty-two pounders, made her a real force to be reckoned with. At over 2,000 tons she was a mighty fighting machine and of course naming her after the reigning monarch was an indication of the pride placed in her by the naval establishment.

In August 1782 she had been ordered to go to Spithead, off the entrance of Portsmouth harbour, so that repairs could be completed and she could be re-provisioned in time to head off to Gibraltar to relieve the siege. Time was of the essence, and there were large but unknown numbers of shipwrights, carpenters and plumbers working on board. They needed to run pipes to a new cistern which was being fitted, necessitating making a hole in the ship's hull.

It must have been crowded – families of crewmen were allowed on board, accounting for perhaps as many as 300 extra personnel. A full complement of 867 sailors was on board, because shore leave had been cancelled as a means of cutting down on the risk of desertion. As an inducement to the men, between 100 and 200 prostitutes had also been allowed to board the ship and were busy plying their trade. There were also a number of peddlers on board, seeking to sell merchandise to the sailors waiting to depart on their next trip, to the Mediterranean.

Early on the morning of 29 August the centre of gravity of the ship was deliberately altered by moving some of the guns into the centre of the ship, so that the hull could be exposed to allow for works to be undertaken on the port side. This meant that the ship was finely balanced and therefore unable to cope when loading operations got under way in the form of barrels of rum, which were put on board on the now-low port side. The ship shifted so that the centre of gravity was tilted, a situation which caused the carpenter to rush to the lieutenant of the watch to ask him urgently to restore equilibrium. Unfortunately, the lieutenant was having none of it, since he wanted the hull repairs finished quickly and saw no danger in the fact that the ship had heeled over to port. Below decks, the sailors enjoyed the sight of water splashing in through the gun ports, sending the vermin swimming for their lives through the incoming waters. Much merriment ensued as they tried to catch the mice and rats.

A second request from the carpenter was turned down, with the irate response that if the carpenter thought that he could do a better job of looking after the ship perhaps he should take charge.... This left the exasperated carpenter no choice but to go direct to the captain. Once the situation had been explained to him, Captain Waghorn agreed to give the order to shift the guns back onto the starboard side, but before the order could be given the ship suddenly keeled over, its low gun-ports on the port side allowing the sea to wash in. In vain, the captain tried to rescue Rear-Admiral Richard Kempenfelt, who was on board in his cabin and was then in his seventies, but found the door to his cabin jammed shut by the door frame which had twisted under the pressure of the ship heeling over.

Below decks, men tried to move the cannon from port to starboard but the steep slope of the decking meant that the guns broke free and cannoned into each other, crushing men and timbers alike. *Royal George* sank within a matter of minutes, drowning over 900 people. The carpenter was initially saved, but he never regained consciousness and died within twenty-four hours. Rather more fortunate was the lieutenant of the watch, who survived unscathed and who was perhaps lucky that in the subsequent court martial there was deemed to be insufficient evidence to hold him responsible. Mind you, with most of the crew dead it was not surprising that there was little conclusive evidence, and there was a general feeling that the ship was old, her timbers were affected by worm, and that the frame was therefore not strong enough to cope with the stresses and strains put on the ship as it was tilted. Besides, the lieutenant may well have been told that he would be 'looked after by the navy' if he agreed not to spill the beans about what happened. In the end he was promoted.

Captain Waghorn survived, unlike Rear-Admiral Kempenfelt, who perished in the disaster. Also killed were three brothers on board the sloop *Swallow*, engaged in loading the brandy barrels. The sloop was caught in the masts and rigging of *Royal George* as she rolled over, taking her to a watery grave.

Many of the people on board were trapped, and the mutilated and bloated bodies started to come to the surface a week or so after the accident. The corpses were simply stripped of anything of value, then a cord was attached to the ankles and the bodies hauled ashore and given a mass burial at various places along the Hampshire coastline.

The ship had sunk in 20 metres of water right in the middle of the harbour and was a hazard to navigation for a number of years. The tips of her masts were visible and at low tide the upper decks were above water. Various attempts were made to try to lift the wreck, or to break it up on site. Efforts to salvage some of the cannon using an early form of diving bell started almost immediately and fifteen cannon were recovered in this way. It was not until 1834 that the Deane brothers started diving on the wreck site, using a special air-fed helmet which allowed them to breathe underwater. Thus equipped, they managed to salvage seven of the massive forty-two pounders, along with twenty-one of the smaller guns. That still left the wreck as a maritime hazard: a colonel in the Royal Engineers was tasked with the problem of salvaging whatever remained of value and of destroying the rest as best he could. Over a four year period, he brought up another thirty cannon as well as bringing up a large section of the keel. The other timbers were blown up in 1840. The pioneering work eventually led to the formation of the Admiralty Salvage Section, and the suits worn by the early divers, although modified, proved of use for another 150 years until more modern suits and breathing apparatus prevailed.

Sometimes the negligence resulted in fire on board ship, one of the worst scenarios a sailor could ever encounter. In Volume One of *The Nautical Magazine: a Journal of*

Papers on Subjects Connected with Maritime Affairs in general the background to the events which had occurred thirty-seven years earlier, off Spithead, was recounted:

> *His Majesty's ship Boyne, of ninety-eight guns, was ordered by letter from the Navy Board dated 3 February 1795.... to have her defects made good at Spithead, and to be stored [i.e. to have stores put on board] for Channel service.... On May-day, in the afternoon, the Boyne, while at anchor was observed to be on fire.*

HMS *Boyne* had been built as a second-rate ship of the line at Woolwich Dockyard, with her keel having been laid down in 1783. Work on her was slow, no doubt influenced by the fact that operations linked to the American War of Independence were beginning to be scaled down. She was a huge ship by the standards of the day – her design was basically the same as HMS *Victory* but with a different allocation and spread of guns over various decks – and her construction took over seven years. She was finally launched on Sunday 27 June 1790.

Manned by a crew of 720 officers, men, boys and marines she was one of four almost identical ships constructed to the same design. Her construction had cost just under £60,000 and, at five years old, *Boyne* had many years of naval service ahead of her. Following a spell operating in the Caribbean she had returned to England and, as was the custom at the time, a number of her cannon on the gun deck were left fully loaded and ready for action, in case of a surprise attack.

It was a brilliant sunny day, and the marines on board were carrying out musket firing practice from a number of positions on the ship. Down in the wardroom the stove was lit to prepare breakfast for the officers, but as luck would have it the flue from the stove ran up through the admiral's quarters to the upper gun deck. As the iron flue heated up it set alight the papers on the desk of Vice-Admiral Jervis. From there the flames spread rapidly throughout the ship; it was too late for anything to be done to extinguish the blaze. Alarmed by the fire, other naval ships in the immediate vicinity slipped their anchors and headed for safety off the Isle of Wight. And as news of the conflagration spread a large number of the local populace gathered to watch. In the words of the *Nautical Magazine* of 1832:

> *The novelty and grandeur of the spectacle attracted together an immense number of spectators, in every place where a view could be obtained; but the curiosity which was at first universally evinced was somewhat cooled when it was found that the guns ... on the lower deck were shotted [i.e. loaded with shot] ... the Boyne being under orders to sail the next day. The consequence was, several shots fell on Southsea beach to the great alarm and discomforture of those who had been attracted to the spot.*

Little damage was caused to the onlookers. Fortunately, most of the 800 sailors on board *Boyne* were rescued, and only eleven persons were killed. However, that was not the end of the commotion; when the heat of the fire set off the loaded cannon, one of the shots managed to strike the navy ship *Queen Charlotte* some distance away, killing two seamen. As the flames spread they reached *Boyne*'s anchor ropes, and once these burned through the helpless ship drifted across Portsmouth Harbour until she reached a sandbar opposite Southsea Castle. The flames finally reached the gunpowder store and a mighty explosion tore the fine ship to pieces.

The story did not finish there: the wreck was to be a hazard to shipping for the next forty years. Then the *Hampshire Telegraph* on 27 June 1840 carried the story that an attempt had been made by a businessman called Mr Abbinett to blow up what remained of the wreck. A party of Royal Sappers and Miners came from Spithead, bringing with them a couple of wrought-iron cylinders, each containing around 300 lbs of gunpowder, along with a voltaic conducting apparatus. 'Two columns of water thrown up were about eight or ten feet high and a great number of fish were killed by both explosions.' The report continued:

After the second explosion Mr. Deane went down again and found that both sides of the wreck, which had stood eight or ten feet high before the explosion, were knocked to pieces and laid prostrate, so that he could walk into the hull, which before was inaccessible from the outside. A deep crater was also formed in the mud alongside. Some pieces of timber and several copper bolts were brought up immediately by Mr. Deane; and we have no doubt that Mr. Abbinett will be well repaid for the expense of gunpowder, &c., by the copper fastenings of the fragments of the wreck which he will be able to recover.

If Spithead was to prove a graveyard for the careless, Plymouth was to prove just as dangerous, as the fate of *Amphion* demonstrates. She had been launched in 1780, a fifth-rate Amazon-class frigate named after a classical Greek hero. Sixteen years into her career she had seen service in Newfoundland and had called back to her home town of Plymouth for repairs to her mast, damaged in a gale coming up the English Channel. She was under the command of Captain Israel Pellew. The harbour was busy and she was moored up alongside a sheer-hulk (in other words a floating platform, comprising what was left of an old ship called *Yarmouth*, used for placing masts in ships under construction or repair).

The work was due to be finished the following day and there were dozens of shipwrights on board. And, since most of the seamen were from Plymouth and its immediate environs, their families had gathered for a chance to see their loved ones on board before the ship sailed.

Captain Pellew had invited a number of colleagues to join him for dinner. It was four in the afternoon and at that stage only his first lieutenant and the English captain of the Dutch vessel *Overijssel* had arrived. It had been the anniversary of the coronation of King George III and earlier in the afternoon a royal salute had boomed out across the harbour. Suddenly a much louder explosion was heard, and within a matter of minutes *Amphion* was sliding bow-first under the water.

Pellew was extraordinarily fortunate to survive what turned out to be an on-board explosion. The first blast had pushed him violently towards the stern window of his cabin. It was followed immediately by a second blast which blew him through the window and into the water. Here he was rescued and taken ashore for treatment to his injuries, which turned out to be largely superficial. Pellew made a full recovery and was eventually made up to admiral and was given command of the seventy-four gun *Conqueror* at the Battle of Trafalgar.

His good fortune was shared by the first lieutenant, who was able to swim to shore unaided. But the captain of the Dutch ship was driven against the side of the cabin with such force that he cracked his skull and drowned. His mutilated corpse was not found until a month later.

The catastrophic explosion destroyed *Amphion* and killed some 278 people on board. Little damage was caused to the old *Yarmouth*, to whom she was tied, although its decks were covered with a macabre pile of the dead and dying and of assorted body parts. The injured were taken to the Royal Hospital but most of them died of their injuries in the coming days. There were fewer than a dozen survivors, including an unharmed young baby, found in the arms of its dead mother.

As to what caused the explosion, the finger of suspicion pointed towards the ship's gunner. He had been observed in town, somewhat the worse for wear as a result of heavy drinking, earlier in the day. He had been suspected of stealing gunpowder and it was thought likely that he had accidentally dropped a small amount of powder near the front magazine. The powder which he dropped then ignited, triggering another explosion a few seconds later when the entire magazine caught fire.

The resulting court martial was unable to establish exactly what happened to cause the explosion, but it was later reported in the press that a sack had been recovered from the bed of the harbour, containing gunpowder covered with a layer of ship's biscuits. This would certainly suggest that the gunner may have stolen the powder with a view to selling it for his own profit. Initially the finger of blame had been pointed at the lieutenant in charge of the front magazine, but evidence was produced to show that the gunner had taken the key to the magazine earlier that day, without the knowledge or permission of the lieutenant.

The city of Plymouth was in shock in the days after the tragedy – everyone knew someone who had perished, and it was many weeks before the river and harbour stopped revealing its gruesome reminders of the tragedy. Immediate attempts had to be made to clear the wreck from the harbour but it was too close to the shore for explosives to be used. An ingenious way of moving the wreck onto the shore was worked out. On 3 October cables were passed under the hull of *Amphion*, bow and stern, and then lashed to the frigates *Castor* and *Iphigenia*, positioned on either side. The frigates had been prepared for the enterprise by being made watertight, with all gun-ports filled in. The two frigates were then filled with water until they were as low in the water as possible. At the lowest point in the tide the ropes were tightened to their utmost, using capstans, and the water in *Castor* and *Iphigenia* was then pumped out. As the tide came in, all three ships, bound together as a single platform, rose in the water and were able to be towed away. *Amphion* was then beached and broken up.

But, if leaving gunpowder lying around was dangerous, spare a thought for the crew of *Queen Charlotte*. She was the same vessel as is mentioned earlier in connection with the explosion on board *Boyne*, when a loose cannon fired a shot killing two of the crew. In 1790 *Queen Charlotte* had been launched, all of 190 ft long and weighing over 2,200 tons. With 100 guns on board she was the second largest vessel then afloat (after *Ville de Paris*, a former French ship captured by the Royal Navy and put to its own use). She had enjoyed an illustrious career, being used as Admiral Howe's flagship in the Battle of the Glorious First of June in 1794 and also playing a part in the (partial) British victory at the Battle of Groix. She was however to come to an ignominious end in 1800, when on 16 March she reached the north Italian port of Livorno (known to the English as Leghorn). She was then the flagship of Vice Admiral Lord Keith and was under the command of Captain James Todd.

The vice admiral was ashore, no doubt enjoying his breakfast, when at 6 a.m. smoke was observed coming from close to the captain's cabin. Fire had broken out when some hay had been placed near a tub in which a slow-burning rope was kept, ready to be used at short notice if the ship was attacked and needed to light the gun fuses. The flames from the burning straw quickly enveloped the main mast and spread to the sails. Fire on board a ship can quickly cause chaos, especially with many of the officers still asleep below decks, and although the crew manned the pumps they were unable to extinguish the rapidly spreading flames. One man emerged as the hero, the 22-year-old Lieutenant Dundas. He led a party of seventy men down below decks and in the frightening conditions of choking, blinding smoke and steam, with fire raining burning wood around their ears, they tried to batten down the hatches and to flood the lower decks to prevent the fire from spreading. For three hours they laboured but by 9 a.m. the middle deck was beginning to burn through and the heavy cannon were crashing down on to the deck below.

Dundas led his men to safety but soon the mizzenmast came crashing down, throwing many men into the water.

The Admiral, on shore watching proceedings, must have been appalled. As the British Register 'State of Public Affairs' for April 1800 makes clear:

Lord Keith being … on shore at Leghorn, had the mortification of discovering the Queen Charlotte on fire four or five leagues at sea. This sight rendered Lord Keith almost frantic – he immediately gave orders for all the vessels and boats to put off, and every assistance to be given; and in this service he was zealously seconded by the Austrian General, and all ranks in Leghorn. They came to an anchor, as the wind blew strongly off the land, but the flames were so rapid that very little hopes could be entertained of saving her.

The would-be rescuers were driven back when the loaded guns on board *Queen Charlotte* started to go off in the searing heat. The blaze was completely out of control and just five hours after the incident with the smouldering hay which started the fire, flames reached the ship's main powder magazine. The entire ship exploded in an enormous fireball, killing 673 officers and men. Dundas survived, and later climbed the naval ladder to the very top, becoming First Naval Lord by the time of his eventual death in 1834.

There were of course other cases of ships being destroyed at sea by fire or explosion, not involving enemy action, but by their very nature there was often nothing left to show what had happened. A case in point was *Ardent*, which disappeared in 1794 in the Mediterranean off the coast of France. She was a third-rate ship, launched some twelve years earlier, carrying sixty-four guns and had been detailed to keep watch on a couple of French frigates. She simply disappeared. Months later in the Gulf of Genoa wreckage was spotted which was believed to have come from *Ardent*. Scorch marks on the recovered part of the quarter deck, together with signs of an explosion, convinced the authorities that she had caught fire and then blown up. Not one of the 500 men on board survived.

Part Four

OTHER CASTAWAYS

Chapter 12

The Wreck of the Batavia

Halfway through the year of 1629 an entry appears in the log kept by a man called Francisco Pelsaert, on board the ship *Batavia*:

FOURTH of JUNE, being Monday morning, on the second day of Whitsuntide, with a clear full moon about two hours before daybreak during the watch of the skipper [Ariaen Jacobsz], I was lying in my bunk feeling ill and felt suddenly, with a rough terrible movement, the bumping of the ship's rudder, and immediately after that I felt the ship held up in her course against the rocks, so that I fell out of my bunk.

Whereon I ran up and discovered that all the sails were in Top, the wind South west, that during the night the course had been north east by North, and that lay right in the middle of a thick spray. Round the ship there was only a little surf, but shortly after that heard the Sea breaking hard round about. I said, 'Skipper, what have you done that through your reckless carelessness you have run this noose round our necks?'

In fact, the ship had struck an island known as Beacon Island in a group of just over 100 islands named earlier by the Portuguese as the Houtman Abrolhos, situated some fifty miles off the western coast of Australia. The ship was on its maiden voyage, having left Texel in the Netherlands eight months previously. The ship was the pride of the Dutch East India Company, known as the VOC, and Francisco Pelsaert was a senior officer of the Company. He was not a sailor, but as the chief representative of the VOC on board the ship he was in charge of the voyage, whereas the skipper, Ariaen Jacobsz, was responsible for day-to-day sailing matters.

On board was a treasure of gold and silver, and numerous antiques and *objets d'art*. Also on board were civilians heading out East to work for the VOC, along with a group of 100 soldiers, an attractive young woman called Lucretia Jans – and a bankrupt pharmacist called Jeronimus Cornelisz. It proved to be an incendiary set of ingredients and it sparked off a story of incredible hardship involving rape, murder and utter depravity, as well as great heroism, bravery and fine seamanship.

Batavia was named after the Dutch capital of what was then the Dutch East Indies (now known as Jakarta, on the island of Java). The ship had been built in the Netherlands in 1627 on the orders of the recently formed VOC at a time when the Dutch were becoming one of the major trading powers in the world. She was over 56 metres long and was intended to carry 341 people (crew and passengers combined). She was protected by twenty-four cast iron cannon to deter pirates.

Up until 1602 each of the Dutch voyages to the Far East involved forming a separate limited company, specifically dealing with the financial arrangements for that one voyage. When the voyage finished, that company would then be wound up and a new one started for the next voyage. But in 1602 the Dutch East India Company was formed in order to arrange successive voyages to and from the Far East. It had the power to raise its own private army, and to issue its own currency. Indeed, the Dutch authorities gave the company quasi-governmental powers, including the ability to wage war, imprison and execute convicts, negotiate treaties, and establish colonies. The company quickly became hugely profitable. It was the world's first multinational company – and became the first company in history to issue bonds and shares of stock to the general public.

The tentacles of the VOC were enormous. The VOC soon established a settlement near the Cape of Good Hope, with its re-fuelling and repairing facilities at Cape Town. The company also controlled settlements along the coast of Madagascar, along the Arabian Gulf, and it established some fifteen trading stations down the west coast of India. From Burma, Thailand, Malaysia, Vietnam and across to Japan the company had significant trading outposts.

The Company's Far Eastern operations were controlled from what is now Indonesia, and for many hundreds of ships their main destination was Batavia, the gateway to the riches of the East. From there the Company could import Asian merchandise, particularly spices such as cloves and nutmeg, and a measure of its success is shown by the fact that in the seventeenth century the Company imported into Europe more than five times the volume of spices than its nearest rival, the British East India Company.

The VOC had first conquered the small Javanese village of Jaya-karta (later, shortened to Jakarta) on the northwest coast of Java in 1619. It did so in order to establish an exclusive port for their trading activities in the Straits of Malacca. The name Batavia was given to it after an area in Holland near Nijmegan and it quickly became a model of Dutch colonial power. City walls encircled it, protecting the numerous warehouses, buildings and residences that lined the straight canals and main roads which divided the city into a neat grid radiating from the shoreline. This European façade hid the fact that the city was unlike any of its European counterparts, with crocodiles infesting the canals. There was inadequate drainage and the pollution was a terrible problem. It was an unhealthy environment, and one which would claim the lives of many of the men and women working for the VOC.

The rewards were however impressive, and there was an opportunity for employees to make money, legally or otherwise, which would have been beyond their dreams back home in the Netherlands. The scale of operations was staggering: in the course of the seventeenth and eighteenth centuries more than one million Europeans found employment working for the Dutch company in its Far East trade and the company was responsible for arranging over 4,700 trips by its own vessels around the Cape and across the Indian Ocean.

To protect the goods stored in the warehouses the VOC maintained a garrison in Batavia and regularly shipped reinforcements out to maintain military numbers. The company also had a need for regular consignments of gold and silver, with which to buy goods from the local traders. In addition, fine quality fancy goods as well as antiques were imported for use as gifts to important local rulers and dignitaries.

In most cases the VOC ships hugged the coast around Southern Africa, passing up through the Madagascar channel, before crossing the Indian Ocean, skirting around the sub-continent, and then reaching Sumatra and the rest of the Dutch East Indies. It was a safe option, but not necessarily the quickest. Sea captains realised that if they headed south from the tip of Africa, deep into the empty expanses of the southern oceans, they could pick up the winds known as the Roaring Forties, carrying them eastward at a fast rate. The lure of the route was that it could cut four weeks off the journey – a very significant saving in terms of both time and money.

The problem, in the days before longitude was established, was that navigators could not be sure how far east they had travelled before turning north, to bring them to Java. Turn too soon and the benefit of the helpful winds would be lost. Leave it too late – as Ariaen Jacobsz on *Batavia* was to do – and a ship could hit the Australian coast. The navigators on board *Batavia* had miscalculated their position by nearly a thousand kilometres. The miscalculation probably arose because they had no accurate way of measuring the effect of ocean swells and currents, and the speed of the wind was variable. Whatever; the result was a disaster and the ship started to break up in the rough seas.

Pelsaert had been unwell throughout the journey, but he knew his duty. It was to protect the company's assets, rather than to save lives. His main duty was to salvage the ten chests of gold and silver held on board and another one overflowing with jewels – intended for use by the merchants in paying for the goods waiting to be returned to Holland. *Batavia* had been expected to bring back a valuable cargo of pepper and cloves, as well as dried indigo plants used for making dye. Also on board had been a valuable Roman cameo and two items from antiquity belonging to the artist Reubens, intended as a gift for the Great Mughal in India.

Pelsaert had enjoyed a somewhat chequered career with the VOC and he would have been anxious to salvage what little remained of his reputation. So, while the passengers and crew were staggering ashore and trying to work out how they were going to survive, Pelsaert got into the nine-metre open longboat, accompanied by skipper Ariaen Jacobs, as well as by the ship's bosun and a mixture of forty-seven crew and passengers. Before they departed they had a quick look around to see if there was a supply of fresh water, but found none. They sailed towards the nearby mainland, but for the next eleven days were unable to locate streams or ponds. At this point the decision was made to travel north to the city of Batavia, a distance of nearly 2,000 miles.

They had left without explaining their plans to the other survivors, so these poor souls, perhaps 225 of them, must have assumed that they were being abandoned. On board the longboat, Pelsaert and his company (men, women and a small child) faced an extraordinary journey. The skipper and bosun may have had some familiarity with the coast, because the Dutch had been travelling past the western coast of Australia for some years. No one knew if the land mass, christened New Holland, was a long island or was part of a new continent, and none of the interior had been explored. However, unlike earlier voyagers, the longboat kept close in to the coast, calling in to the shore on various occasions in a fruitless search for water and fresh provisions. Eventually, after eleven days, they made landfall and found a creek enabling them to fill buckets with water. They also encountered aborigines, who ran away. They continued their voyage, spending an incredible thirty-three days and nights on board, exposed to all weathers. They had no charts, and as Pelsaert was ill for most of the journey the task of maintaining spirits and morale lay with the skipper. Passengers were limited to consuming just half a pint of water per day, together with a very small amount of bread. Amazingly, not one single person died during the epic journey.

The extraordinary thing was that they made such good time that they reached Batavia only a matter of days after the arrival of the other six ships which had set out as a flotilla from the Netherlands all those months earlier. The others had kept to the traditional route around India, unwilling to try their luck with the Roaring Forties.

The Governor General in charge of Batavia Province was not best pleased to hear that Pelsaert had failed to secure the assets of the company, and that the money and jewellery were probably scattered on the ocean floor. He ordered Pelsaert to head back to salvage the company possessions – and, almost as an afterthought, to rescue the remaining personnel.

First, the bosun was taken off, and charged with negligently allowing the shipwreck to happen. He was to be the scapegoat, and he paid with his life, executed for his 'outrageous behaviour'. The skipper was more fortunate. At that stage little was known about his very questionable involvement in the events which led to the wreck, and although he was arrested and charged with negligence, for now he was spared.

Pelsaert was put in command of the rescue ship *Sardam*. The Governor General made it clear that time was not an object – the recovery could take as long as it took to get back everything and there was a strong hint that only complete success would spare Pelsaert from being punished. Ironically it was a voyage which was to take over sixty days (nearly double the first leg) meaning that they had been away for almost four months. Put simply, they were unable to find the archipelago of low-lying islands where the ship *Batavia* had been wrecked, and it must have been some relief when they finally reached the Houtman Abrolhos archipelago and located the survivors on 17 September 1629. What they found when they got there was a horrific story of bloodshed, rape and murder.

To understand what had happened it is necessary to go back to events in Holland in the years leading up to the voyage, and to look at the relationship between Pelsaert and the skipper, and at the behaviour of one of the passengers, the failed pharmacist Jeronimus Cornelisz.

Pelsaert, despite being a senior figure in the VOC world, had never really excelled in office. He was a renowned womaniser and one time when he was working in the Indian city of Agra, he managed to seduce one of the mistresses of the Great Mughal. One night she slipped round to his quarters, and while he was out of the room helped herself to a glass of what she thought was wine, from a large container. Unfortunately for her it was neat oil of cloves – something which the human body finds poisonous, and can lead to seizures and breathing difficulties. She suffered burns to the oesophagus, went into a coma, and died shortly afterwards. As can be imagined, that took some explaining to the most powerful ruler in India, and Pelsaert's career never really recovered.

Pelsaert did not get on well with the man chosen to skipper *Batavia*. There had been a run-in some years before when Pelsaert allegedly gave Jacobsz a public dressing-down in front of other merchants, after Jacobsz had insulted the wife of his superior. Pelsaert may have forgotten the incident, but it left Jacobsz fuming, and determined to get his revenge.

The other piece in the jigsaw was Jeronimus Cornelisz. Here was a man whose life had fallen to pieces following the tragic death of his baby son. The mother of the child was unwell and the baby was farmed out to be wet-nursed. But the child died shortly afterwards – of syphilis. The wet-nurse was adamant that the child had caught the disease from its mother, which was a grossly defamatory suggestion and one which Cornelisz was bound to deny. He sought redress through the courts, and in doing so neglected his business. His creditors called in their loans and seized his pharmacy premises and goods. Faced with bankruptcy and public humiliation, Cornelisz went to pieces. He joined a religious sect which was considered both heretical and dangerous. It may well have been part of a movement called the Church of the Rose Cross. Many viewed it as being satanic, and certainly it was vehemently opposed by the Dutch authorities. It is unclear exactly *what* Cornelisz believed in, but it seems to have involved the convenient idea that if a man thought of an idea and wanted to act on it, that was fine and dandy because the idea would have been put into the man's mind by God, and acting on the idea was merely carrying out God's will.

Cornelisz enrolled as a junior officer on board *Batavia*, intent on making a new start in life, but he brought with him on board his thirst for redress against a cruel world, and the attitude that any way of achieving that redress was acceptable because it had divine approval. Cornelisz found an ally in the skipper and the pair discussed a scheme to start a mutiny on board *Batavia*, aimed at taking over the ship, absconding with all the treasure and then pursuing a life of wealth and opulence as pirates.

The plan developed after *Batavia* left Cape Town. As mentioned, there was originally a flotilla involving six other ships, but four of them went in a different direction. The two remaining ships in the loose convoy were soon shaken off, leaving the plotters to plan their next step. They needed to know that a number of the sailors on board would join the planned mutiny as it was not something they could implement on their own. To that end they hit upon the idea of provoking Pelsaert into punishing the entire crew, in circumstances where this would be perceived as being unfair and harsh.

Since there was a rather attractive woman on board in the form of Lucretia Jans, they decided to provoke a reaction from Pelsaert by carrying out a particularly vulgar and unpleasant assault on the poor woman. The attack took place at night, with the men wearing masked disguises. As expected, she rushed back to the Great Cabin to inform Pelsaert of the attack, but to the dismay of the attackers she was able to identify the individuals who had carried out the assault. She had seen through their disguises and identified one of them from his voice. This scuppered the plans of the would-be mutineers, because it meant that there was to be no indiscriminate punishment involving the entire crew. Indeed, rather strangely, the sickly Pelsaert took no action at all, having decided to defer punishment until after the ship had reached its destination.

Frustrated in their plans to embark on a life of piracy, Jacobsz and Cornelisz were forced to bide their time, but the shipwreck, when it finally came, created a power vacuum in which they were able to make their move. For Cornelisz it may have been a dream to become ruler of a new kingdom, based in New Holland, backed with all the looted treasure. For Jacobsz it may have been his plan to lie in wait for the rescue ship which was bound to come for them, and then to use it to embark on a life of piracy on the high seas, lying in wait for wealthy merchantmen trading in exotic and expensive goods.

This, then, was the background to the appalling events which followed the wrecking of *Batavia*, on the jagged rocks and coral reef in the shallow waters off Beacon Island. The ship did not sink, and lay, its back broken, in the shallows. It is thought that forty people drowned in the first few hours, leaving the others to wade ashore. There they found that Cornelisz was the acting senior officer, following the departure of Pelsaert, the captain and the bosun. Cornelisz quickly realised that there were too many mouths to feed, and that if he was to succeed in his plans he would need to whittle down the numbers so that only his own supporters remained.

Beacon Island was barren and lacking in water. It was separated from two nearby islands known as East and West Wallabi and was also within viewing distance of Seal Island. Cornelisz sent a party of men, women and cabin boys to Seal Island, claiming that there was water to be found there. He knew full well that this was highly unlikely but must have been astonished to see figures still moving around on the island some weeks later. Cornelisz sent a group of his supporters to 'take care' of the situation: they did so, and everyone on the island was butchered.

Cornelisz had a particular concern with the VOC soldiers. These were not trained military men, but inexperienced youngsters on their way to perform garrison duties on a five-year posting. There were no officers, and Cornelisz ordered them to surrender their weapons. He was particularly worried about one of the soldiers, a youngster called Wiebbe Hayes. He was a natural leader and in the aftermath of the wreck had organised the construction of shelters, the distribution of supplies and so on. He had used a small section of sail as both a wind break and as a means of collecting whatever rain water might fall, funnelling it into a barrel used for collection purposes. He was the go-to man for all the shipwrecked passengers, someone who commanded respect and who was therefore a direct threat to Cornelisz.

Not a lot is known about young Hayes. He was probably 21 at the time and heralded from Frisia in the Netherlands. He was reasonably well educated and could read and write. In all likelihood he came from a poor but respectable family.

To get him out of the way, Cornelisz ordered Hayes to take the soldiers on what he thought would be a fool's errand – a trip over to West Wallabi island. A series of smoke signals were agreed upon, to show whether Hayes was successful in his quest for water on the island. Given that Cornelisz never expected for one moment that they would succeed it must have been something of a shock, some twenty days later, when he observed the signal to show that water had been located. As it happens this was not on West Wallabi but on its neighbour, East Wallabi. In fact, the soldiers had not only found a natural water cistern, but the island was inhabited by small mammals such as Tammar wallabies. Although they had surrendered their guns, the men were at least able to catch the animals and survive in relative comfort.

The Tammar wallaby is about the size of a rabbit and has the unique ability of being able to drink sea water. There were also birds, eggs, and such plentiful supplies of fish that one of the survivors later claimed that they could catch forty fish the size of a large cod in the space of a single hour. Another survivor wrote: 'The Lord our God fed us so richly that we could have lived there with ten thousand men for a hundred years.'

Conditions back on Beacon Island were nothing like as favourable. Cornelisz gave the signal for the men to return, but by then Hayes had got to know of his treachery. Presumably he had got to learn of the massacre on Seal Island, and it made him realise that his men were liable to be attacked. He organised the men to build a small defensive fort – the very first building to be constructed by Europeans on what is now Australian soil – and to make weapons with which to defend themselves. Rocks for throwing were lined up, and simple pikes were constructed out of metal spikes lashed to wooden spars salvaged from the ship. Wiebbe Hayes reasoned that the only access to the island was over the mudflats on one side of the island.

All other approaches were impassable because of the encircling coral reef and therefore Hayes placed lookouts by the edge of the mudflats.

Back on Beacon, Cornelisz pursued his evil plans, ordering his supporters to murder anyone who opposed him. The women were forced to become sex slaves, with the attractive Lucretia Jans being saved as bed-companion for his exclusive use. Families would be sent off on fishing expeditions, and as soon as they were out of sight of the others on the island they would be thrown overboard to drown. Others had their throats slit as they lay asleep. Always the murders were carried out on the express orders of Cornelisz, but never actually by him personally. One such order was that all the sick and infirm should be killed. Over a period of six weeks some 120 people were murdered.

Cornelisz was confident that at some stage the VOC would send a vessel to retrieve the sunken treasure. Only one of the boxes had been recovered at that stage, but the rest were easy to access at the appropriate time. Cornelisz planned to lay a trap for the rescue ship and then to overcome the captain and crew, and to flee the island with the treasure. Hayes was the only fly in the ointment, since there would be a real danger that he would alert the rescue party to what was happening. Cornelisz knew that he had to eradicate Hayes and his group of perhaps forty-five soldiers on East Wallabi. He was however up against a group who were better fed, had high morale, and were led by a man with far greater leadership qualities that Cornelisz could ever aspire to. Besides, the soldiers knew that they either fought or died.

Cornelisz sent twenty men to try and take East Wallabi, but the attackers were met with a fusillade of rocks and were forced to withdraw. A month passed before Cornelisz decided to lead a second attack, this time with him in command. First, he sent a small group ashore to try and negotiate a peaceful outcome, offering blankets and clothing to Hayes and his men, in return for fresh food and water. He then made a fatal mistake by heading a party of five men as they waded ashore and attempted to bribe the defending soldiers with offers of large cash sums. This was exactly what Hayes was expecting from Cornelisz, and led him into a trap. By that time Cornelisz must have been a curious sight. He had previously broken into Pelsaert's luggage, and helped himself to items of finery, such as a gold-trimmed jacket. Dripping with jewels he must have assumed that 'clothes maketh the man' and that the ragged and unkempt soldiers would immediately recognize his innate superiority. They did not, and promptly tied him up. Cornelisz, looking like a character from a comic opera, was then tossed into a deep pit and for three weeks was given the thankless task of plucking sea birds which were thrown down to him. He was permitted to eat every ninth bird thrown down to him – raw – since he had no means of cooking them.

The other four supporters who had tried to storm the island with Cornelisz were rounded up and killed, leaving the rest of the mutineers to beat a hasty retreat to

Beacon Island. There, they elected a new leader, one Wouter Loos. The mutineers decided to mount a new attack – and this time they brought with them a couple of guns salvaged from *Batavia*. For a couple of hours, they kept out of range of the barrage of rocks being hurled at them and managed to pick off several of the defenders, one at a time. It was obviously going to be a fight with only one possible outcome: rocks versus guns was never going to be an equal contest.

But then an event occurred which changed everything. A ship appeared. It was *Sardam* with Pelsaert on board. There followed a mad scramble as to who could reach the *Sardam* first to give their side of the story. In the case of Wiebbe Hayes it meant sprinting a couple of miles along the length of the island, getting into a small rowing boat, and rowing out to the ship. For the mutineers it meant a somewhat longer rowing distance, and they lacked the determination of Hayes, who won the rather odd biathlon with a couple of minutes to spare.

He had barely acquainted Pelsaert with the facts before the mutineers arrived with their version of events. They claimed that Hayes was not to be trusted and that it was Hayes who had carried out the murders. But for Pelsaert it was not hard to discover the villains, because there in the bottom of the boat were all the cutlasses and other weapons. Besides, they were all wearing sundry items of clothing stolen from Pelsaert's cabin. As Pelsaert later wrote in the Journal:

When they came over, we immediately took them prisoner, and we forthwith began to examine them, especially a certain Jan Hendrixs from Bremen – who immediately confessed that he had murdered and helped to murder 17 to 20 people, under the order of Jeronimus Cornelis [sic]. I asked him the origin and circumstances of this, and why had they practiced such cruelties. He said that he also wished to explain how it had all started, – saying, that the skipper Ariaen Jacobs, together with Jeronimus Cornelis, the bosun and still more others, had it in mind to seize the ship Batavia before it was wrecked; that they had intended to kill the Commander [Pelsaert] and most of the people on board, and to throw the dead into the sea and then to go pirating with the ship.

Further interrogations of the mutineers followed, enabling Pelsaert to piece together the planned hijacking of *Batavia* and later of *Sardam*. Pelsaert was of course astounded at the rapes and murders, but equally was incandescent with rage at the affront to his personal dignity due to the seizure of his own clothes and personal belongings. Cornelisz was hauled out of the pit and questioned at length, following which Pelsaert summoned a formal court at which Cornelisz was tried for his crimes. It must have been a curious sight, with Cornelisz bloody and stinking after having spent twenty-one days in a dark hole, without sanitation. His defence to the charges was that he had not personally murdered anyone, and that the butchery was the work of others. However, there was some evidence that he may have used his skills as an apothecary to administer poison to a young baby who was crying and causing a disturbance. There was no escaping the fact that Cornelisz had got his men to sign an oath of allegiance to him. There it was, in black and white: he was the leader, and his men were simply carrying out his orders.

His guilt was considered to have been proved. Before sentence of death was carried out his hands were chopped off and he was strung up from gallows erected for the purpose. Three of his four accomplices were hanged without amputation, while another four lost their right hands before joining Cornelisz on the gallows. Gruesome it may have been, but it was on a par with the treatment of similar crimes at the time and was intended as a deterrent to others.

It was Pelsaert's intention to take the other survivors, mutineers and victims alike, back to Batavia. In particular, he took no action at that stage against Wouter Loos, who later was identified as the interim leader, and a boy called Jan Pelgram who, at 18, was considered too young to be hanged. Pelsaert's attention turned to retrieving the treasure. As stated, one chest had already been retrieved and eight of the other nine were soon located by divers and brought to the surface. This was probably easier said than done, as it involved free divers having to work on sharp corals and swirling surf. The tenth treasure chest proved irretrievable, as it was wedged under one of the cast iron cannons resting against the ship's anchor. The decision was made to cut their losses and return to Batavia and on 16 November 1629 *Sardam* finally departed from Abrolhos Archipelago and headed for home.

There was one further event along the way which indicated that being cast away was a punishment meted out not just by pirates but by ordinary sailors and traders: one of the surviving sex slaves gave evidence against Loos and Pelgram. Pelsaert decided to make landfall, where smoke from fires showed that there were aborigines in the area. Loos and Pelgram were put ashore, with a few supplies and a small boat at the entrance to Witticarra Gully, near the present town of Kabarri. Nothing is known of their subsequent fate, but there are stories that they became integrated into the aboriginal community, becoming the first permanent European settlers on Australia.

When Pelsaert reached Batavia, allegations were made against the unfortunate Lucretia Jans. Perhaps other survivors felt that she had a cushy time because of her association with Cornelisz. She was charged with encouraging evil and conspiracy to murder but was acquitted for lack of information. She returned to the Netherlands in 1635.

Six other survivors were tried, found guilty and hanged. The captain, Ariaen Jacobsz, is believed to have died in captivity while consigned to the horrors of the dungeons at the fort at Batavia. The only person to emerge with any credit was Wiebbe Hayes. Pelsaert had promoted him to the rank of sergeant and doubled his wages and on reaching Batavia he was decorated and given the rank of lieutenant, with another substantial pay rise. After that, he disappeared from VOC records and nothing is known as to what became of him. It is, however, worth remembering that the life expectancy of men sent to this Eastern outpost was probably only three years and he may well have died while serving overseas.

Pelsaert was excused from any blame for the original loss, which was not surprising given that he was not a sailor. He was instead appointed to the High Council at Batavia in 1629, but there is no record that he attended any meetings. The Company was happy to post him to Sumatra, regarded as a really dead-end appointment, and he died barely a year later in September 1630. He was probably just 35 years old, although some records put him at 39 when he died. In 1643 his journal was published in Holland. It was to be 1963 before it was translated into English.

In 1647, the mutiny was described in the publication *Ongeluckige voyagie van 't schip Batavia*, based on the trial. This put the blame squarely on the fact that there were so many females on board. It led to a change in the law and limited the numbers of women allowed to be carried on board VOC shipping.

The atrocities were soon forgotten but interest was revived in the 1970s when divers started to bring up some of the artefacts scattered on the ocean floor. Large items, such as the cannon, anchors and ornamental stonework, were brought to the surface, along with smaller artefacts such as coins, drinking vessels, mortars and other household effects. On the islands, mass graves have been located, and the site has been declared part of Western Australia's Museum Wreck Trail. It is described as being part of the country's 'museum without walls' concept.

The events have led to various television films being made and in 1985 the decision was made to build a replica of *Batavia*, to heighten public awareness. It was built by master-shipbuilder Willem Vos at his shipyard at Lelystad. The project took ten years and the ship was finally launched in April 1995, in good time to be taken out to Sydney to be used as the flagship for the Dutch team attending the 2000 Olympic Games.

An opera was written about the shipwreck, entitled *Batavia*, and was premiered in May 2001 at the State Theatre in Melbourne. Radio dramas, articles and books have followed, and the story of a most astonishing story of shipwreck and survival is at last being recognised.

Chapter 13

Philip Ashton

There are of course many reasons why men became stranded on distant shores. It was not just mountainous seas, violent storms, bad seamanship or inaccurate charts. In the century up to 1780 there was also the very real risk of being marooned by pirates. One such example occurred in 1722, off the coast of Massachusetts, involving a young fisherman called Philip Ashton. For a while he became famous after a book describing his exploits was published, under the title of *A History of the Strange Adventures and Signal Deliverances of Mr Philip Ashton Who, After he had made his escape from PIRATES, lived alone on a Desolate Island for about 16 months.* It was published in 1725, building on the success of *Robinson Crusoe* by feeding the insatiable public demand for more and more tales of survival and hardship.

Ashton was 19 years old. He was a sailor who lived at Marblehead, earning a living in the coastal waters near his home. In his own words, his adventure started 'On Friday the 15th of June 1722, after being out some time in a schooner with four men and a boy, off Cape Sable, I stood in for Port Rossaway, designing to lie there all Sunday.'

He was in a small flotilla of over a dozen fishing boats, and in the course of the next few hours every single one of them was boarded and robbed by pirates operating from a brigantine belonging to the infamous Edward Low. Ashton would almost certainly have known Low by his reputation, as he was one of the most barbaric and savage men ever to fly the pirate flag. Those lucky enough to survive an encounter with Low described being tortured, cast adrift without supplies, and being forced to endure indescribable humiliations and hardship. Here was a sadist, who revelled in his reputation for cruelty. The writer Sir Arthur Conan Doyle later described Low as 'savage and desperate', and a man of 'amazing and grotesque brutality'. The New York Times called him a torturer, whose methods would have 'done credit to the ingenuity of the Spanish Inquisition in its darkest days'. During the course of his career he is believed to have captured over 100 merchant ships, while flying his own personal version of the pirate flag, showing a red skeleton on a black background. He was not the sort of man you hoped to encounter on a dark day.

Low needed more hands on board, and when he captured Ashton he sought to enlist him as a crew member. As Ashton himself wrote:

When carried on board the brigantine, I found myself in the hands of Ned Low, an infamous pirate, whose vessel had two great guns, four swivels, and about forty-two men. I was strongly urged to sign the articles of agreement among the pirates, and to join their number, which I steadily refused, and suffered much bad usage in consequence.

Low tried to browbeat and then torture Ashton into agreeing to become an outlaw and to accept the pirate code. He refused, even at gunpoint. Some of Ashton's fellow-fishermen were fortunate. Low had them put ashore because he had a curious rule that he never tried to enlist married men. Ashton was not so lucky and was one of eight men put on board the brigantine and kept under lock and key. He was whipped regularly. The story of Ashton's capture was soon reported in the local papers, with the *Boston News Letter* listing him as one of those captured, in its edition of 9 July, 1722.

Low set sail for the Caribbean, stopping and robbing a number of ships along the way. They paused at the island of Tobago to re-provision, before heading for the South American mainland. By then Low had become the poster boy of the pirate age – the man who everyone wanted to capture and bring to trial. During this voyage the pirate ship was nearly cornered by a French vessel hunting down smugglers. They also had a narrow escape when an English man-o'-war gave chase, but Low escaped when the pursuer ran aground on a sandbank, allowing Low to slip away unhindered.

Ashton may have been a prisoner, but he would have known full well that if their ship had been captured he would almost certainly be sent to the gallows. His guilt would have been assumed from the company he kept. It made Ashton determined to escape at the earliest opportunity, once they arrived at the island of Roatan. It is about fifty miles long and only a couple of miles across and is situated about forty miles off the coast of Honduras. There was no permanent settlement on the island at that time.

In Ashton's words:

Roatan harbour, as all about the Bay of Honduras, is full of small islands, which pass under the general name of Keys; and having got in here, Low, with some of his chief men, landed on a small island, which they called Port Royal Key. There they erected huts and continued carousing and drinking.

He continued:

On Saturday the 9th of March 1723, the cooper, with six hands, in the long-boat, was going ashore for water; and coming alongside of the schooner, I requested to be included as one of the party. Seeing him hesitate, I urged that I had never hitherto been ashore, and thought it hard to be so closely confined, when every one besides had the liberty of landing. The cooper at length took me into the long-boat, while Low, and his chief people, were on a different island from Roatan, where the watering place lay; my only clothing was an Osnaburgh frock and trowsers, a milled cap, but neither shirt, shoes, stockings, nor anything else.

'Osnaburgh' was a type of coarse woven cotton, and 'frock' meant a type of jacket, like a smock. The point was that Ashton had not prepared for an escape and therefore he had no knife, no tools of any sort. In the absence of a flintlock he had no way of cooking or lighting a fire. Ashton went on to explain:

When we first landed, I was very active in assisting to get the casks out of the boat, and in rolling them to the watering-place. Then taking a hearty draught of water, I strolled along the beach, picking up stones and shells; but on reaching the distance of a musket-shot from the party, I began to withdraw towards the skirts of the woods. In answer to a question by the cooper of whither I was going? I replied: 'for cocoa nuts, as some cocoa trees were just before me' and as soon as I was out of sight of my companions, I took to my heels, running as fast as the thickness of the bushes and my naked feet would admit. Notwithstanding I had got a considerable way into the woods, I was still so near as to hear the voices of the party if they spoke loud, and I lay close in a thicket where I knew they could not find me.

Ashton had come ashore towards the eastern tip of the island, in an area now known as Port Royal. He watched as the shore party gave up looking for him, and as he wrote afterwards: 'Thus I was left on a desolate island, destitute of all help, and remote from the track of navigators; but compared with the state and society I had quitted, I considered the wilderness hospitable, and the solitude interesting.'

Even today, the area around Port Royal might be much as Ashton found it in 1723. There is only a sliver of beach leading to the small creeks that flow down from the hills. Moving even a few steps away from the shore, the landscape becomes a tangle of branches, palm trees, and thick vines. Ashton recalled in his narrative that it was 'so prodigiously thick with an underbrush that "tis difficult passing'.

Over the coming days Ashton took stock of the island. It had fresh water and although it had tortoises and wild pigs, Ashton had no way of cutting up meat, even if he could catch an animal. He located turtle eggs buried in the sand, which he ate raw. Fruit was to be his staple diet for the next sixteen months. He picked and ate coco plums and hog plums. He also found sapote fruit lying on the ground. These brown, furry fruit were about the size of a pear and at first Ashton was reluctant to try them in case they were poisonous. However, he decided that they were safe to eat once he saw that the wild hogs were eagerly consuming them. He then announced that the sapote fruit was 'very delicious'.

He had rather more reason to be cautious with what he termed the 'Mangeneil Apple'. Manchineels may resemble an apple at first glance, but these 'noxious fruit' contain an irritant which can burn the skin, or indeed the throat if swallowed. Ashton was wise to avoid the temptation to try them, writing 'I often took up in my hands, and looked upon, but had not the power to eat.' Abstaining from eating manchineels was certainly a wise choice. Ashton explained his daily routine:

It was my daily practice to ramble from one part of the island to another, though I had a more special home near the water-side. Here I built a hut to defend me against the heat of the sun by day, and the heavy dews by night. Taking some of the best branches which I could find fallen from the trees, I contrived to fix them against a low hanging bough, by fastening them together with split palmeto leaves; next I covered the whole with some of the largest and most suitable leaves that I could get. Many of these huts were constructed by me, generally near the beach, with the open part, fronting the sea, to have the better look-out, and the advantage of the sea-breeze, which both the heat and the vermin required.

By 'vermin' Ashton meant the bugs, sand flies and mosquitos which made his life a misery. These crude shelters offered little protection from the insects which Ashton said 'grew so troublesome to me that I was put upon contrivance to get rid of their company.' Ashton's solution was to spend most of the day sitting on one of the small cays that lie just off the island's shore. Using a bamboo pole as a float (he barely knew how to swim), Ashton kicked his way out to the cay, where he could sleep or gaze out at the sea in peace, the constant breeze keeping the bugs away.

On one occasion he lost his bamboo float, and on another was attacked by a shark. He also encountered alligators, and back on the main island was chased by a wild boar. He ended up taking refuge at the top of a tall tree and had to wait for the boar to lose interest. One of the other problems he faced was that he had no footwear and he was to complain bitterly that the sharp rocks, coral and sea shells were lacerating his feet. Presumably only the sea water would stop the bleeding.

Sometime in November 1723, Ashton saw a small canoe approaching with a single man. He was to write: 'the sight excited little emotion. I kept my seat on the beach, thinking I could not expect a friend, and knowing that I had no enemy to fear, nor was I capable of resisting one'.

It turned out that the visitor was British and was on the run from the Spanish. He had decided to come to the island and to live rough by hunting and shooting wild boar and deer. Apparently, the man stayed with Ashton for three days and then, leaving his musket, ammunition and his flintlock behind, wandered off into the jungle to explore the island. He never came back. As a result, Ashton became the proud owner of a canoe, along with a gun and the means to start a fire. Life became considerably easier, because he was now able to cook and eat turtle meat, but it is difficult to avoid the suspicion that Ashton may have killed his new companion, and the story of the visitor 'doing a Captain Oates' may be somewhat unlikely. There is, however, a suggestion that the visitor was swept away in a storm, but in that case, Ashton was extremely fortunate to have been able to salvage the canoe, gun and the wherewithal to light a fire.

As conditions improved, Ashton was to write: 'Here I lived, if it may be called living, alone for about seven months, after losing my British companion. My time was spent in the usual manner, hunting for food, and ranging among the islands.' Eventually, in June 1724, a band of logwood cutters from the mainland appeared off shore when Ashton was sitting by his fire on the beach. The Baymen, as they were called, introduced themselves and, paraphrasing what Ashton wrote, he gave the strangers a brief account of his escape from Low, and his lonely residence for sixteen months, all except three days, the hardships he had suffered, and the dangers to which he had been exposed. Ashton wrote:

They stood amazed at the recital; they wondered I was alive, and expressed much satisfaction at being able to relieve me. Observing me very weak and depressed, they gave me about a spoonful of rum to recruit my fainting spirits; but even this small quantity, from my long disuse of strong liquors, threw me into violent agitation, and produced a kind of stupor, which at last ended in privation of sense. Some of the party perceiving a state of insensibility come on, would have administered more rum, which those better skilled among them prevented; and after lying a short time in a fit, I revived.

In time he recovered and the Baymen took him to another island nearby and gave him food, clothing and shelter.

Ashton stayed with the Baymen for a couple of months, during which time they had a narrow escape from pirates. Ironically, the pirates turned out to be the very same group which had previously caught Ashton and brought him to Roatan. This time, Ashton and his accomplices escaped into the dense undergrowth and waited for the pirates to leave.

Ashton's sixteen-month long ordeal on Roatan came to an end in March 1725. He spotted a passing merchant vessel and when it was forced to take shelter off Roatan during a fierce storm Ashton emerged from the jungle onto the beach to welcome them. He quickly secured a passage home on the ship, called *Diamond* and operating out of Salem, Massachusetts. Ashton was to write of the experience with the words:

By the providence of Heaven we passed safely through the Gulf of Florida, and reached Salem Harbour on the first of May, two years, ten months and fifteen days after I was first taken by pirates; and two years, and two months, after making my escape from them on Roatan island. That same evening I went to my father's house, where I was received as one risen from the dead.

Having recovered from his ordeal Ashton wrote up his account and for a while enjoyed fame as 'the American Crusoe'. He continued to live in Marblehead and in December 1727 married Jane Gallison. She died one year later after giving birth to a daughter. He then married again, to Sarah Bartlett, in July 1729, and went on to have half a dozen children. To end the story with Ashton's own words:

In saving me from the rage of pirates, and the malice of Spaniards, from the beasts of the field, and the monsters of the sea, in keeping me alive amid so many deaths in such a lonely and helpless condition, and in bringing about my deliverance…. And a vessel bound to my own home must come and take me in, I cannot but take notice of the strange concurrence of Divine Providence throughout it all.

Chapter 14

Leendert Hasenbosch

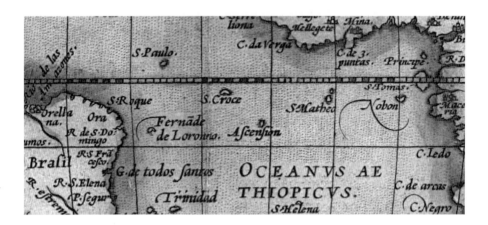

On 6 December 1725 two ships belonging to the Dutch East India Company set sail from Cape Town, heading North towards England. The ships were *James and Mary* and *Compton*, under the respective commands of Captain John Balchen and William Morson. When the ships got as far as the remote and uninhabited Ascension Island, in the South Atlantic, they called in. Balchen wrote in the ship's log:

> *20 January 1726: Anchored on the NW side of the Island Asscesion… here is a fine sandy bay and good landing… sent our boat shore to Turn Turtles… this morning the boat returned with two… Here we found a tent with Bedding and Several Books with some writings by which we find there was a Dutch man turned on Shore here out of a Dutch ship for being guilty of Sodomy in Last May. Could not find him so believed he perished for want of water…*

A corresponding entry appears in the log for *James and Mary*, and it is worth noting that in both cases the skeleton of the unnamed Dutch man was nowhere to be seen. The journal kept by the missing Dutchman was presumably retrieved and brought back to London where Captain Balchen showed it to people with contacts in the world of publishing. Later that year a translation from the Dutch into English appeared, and the resulting publication entitled *Sodomy Punish'd* was published by

John Loveday in 1726. The full title, shown on the frontispiece, stated that the Dutchman bore the name 'Leondert Hussenlosch'.

The preface to that first version opens with a reference to the fact that there had been a recent trial for sodomy in Britain, and continues with the following words:

> *It can't but be pleasing to the Greatest Part of Mankind to peruse the following Pages, since they are Passages which Occurr'd to an unhappy Wretch who, for the same crime was by Order of the Dutch fleet, May 5th 1724, Exposed to the Severity of Want and Hardship on a Desolate Island called Ascension, about 9 degrees South latitude, where 'tis probable he perish'd for want of Necessaries.*

The preface goes on to assert that the journal was found in a trunk the previous January by sailors on board the *James and Mary*. To emphasise the message of sin being punishable by death, the preface ends with the words:

> *May his Calamities with the other Examples of Punishment, for this detested crime, so Present with us, be a Warning to all who have been any ways Guilty to repent, and others who may be unhappily deluded to beware how they are seduc'd to commit this obnoxious sin to God and Nature, a Sin so dreadful in its Consequence both to themselves and others attended with utter shame and ruin here, and with the Infinite Wrath of an offended God in the World to come.*

The reference to the crime of sodomy being 'so present with us' and to a recent sodomy trial arose out of a police raid on premises kept by a woman called Margaret Clapp in Field Lane, Holborn. Mother Clapp, as she was known, kept what was called a 'molly house', where homosexual men could meet. In February 1726 the raid led to a number of men being charged with gross indecency, punishable with fines, imprisonment and a spell in the pillory. For three of the men who were caught, they faced a trial for sodomy, were found guilty and were hanged at Tyburn.

Two years later a different version of the journal appeared, under the title of *An Authentick Relation of the Many Hardships and Sufferings of a Dutch Sailor*. In this version, the identity of the writer was not disclosed. To add to the confusion, the 1728 version stated that the original journal, in Dutch, had been found alongside the skeleton of its author. It also stated that the original of the journal could be inspected at the offices of the publisher. In fact, the suggestion that the diary was found alongside the author's skeleton was a total invention, intended to embellish the story.

A third version was published in 1730, under the title of *The Just Vengeance of Heaven Exemplify'd*. After that, there was no mention of the original journal, and it has remained lost to the present day. The three versions of the story of a shipwrecked Dutchman differ in several important respects. In particular the later versions contain lengthy passages of introspection, with frequent references to the 'abominable practice' of sodomy. Some of the moralistic passages were laid on as if by a trowel: the Dutchman got what he deserved because of his repulsive actions. The finger-wagging was very obviously added to the original manuscript, to suit a particular agenda, and in recent years many have speculated as to the identity of the author of the extra passages. Even Daniel Defoe has been suspected of embroidering all or part of the journal.

More recently, the waters have been further muddied by the 1976 publication of a book by Peter Agnos entitled *The Queer Dutchman*. It turned out to be a work of fiction, not fact, with various invented characters and events, and did nothing to establish the truth of what actually happened in the Ascension Islands 300 years ago.

It is however certain that there is an underlying element of truth to the journal; in 2002 the Dutch historian Michiel Koolbergen established beyond doubt that the man's name was Leendert Hasenbosch, a 30-year-old Dutch sailor. Koolbergen wrote up the story of his meticulous work in *Een Hollandse Robinson Crusoe*, published after Koolbergen's death in 2002.

So, who was Leendert Hasenbosch the sodomitical Dutchman who kept a journal and who died towards the end of 1725? Leendert was on his way back from Batavia (modern day Jakarta) in the Dutch East Indies on board the Dutch ship *Prattenburg*. He had gone out East in 1714 in the employ of the Company as a soldier, and later became a book-keeper. He was still employed as a book-keeper on his return journey, at a salary of sixteen guilders a month. The salary records of the East India Company contain this entry: 'On 17 April 1725, on the *Prattenburg*, he was sentenced to be set ashore, being a villain, on the island of Ascension or elsewhere, with confiscation of his outstanding salary.'

Cast ashore at what is now known as Clarence Bay on 5 May 1725, he was not totally without means of support. He had with him a cask of water, two buckets, an old frying pan, some provisions, bedding, a lamp, a Bible and some other materials including paper and a pen. He had his musket, but no powder or shot, and he was able to take ashore a knife and a small hatchet.

His first diary entry records that he put up a tent, a shelter made of a canvas sheet, on the beach. He had been told it was the time of year when other ships could be expected to pass by, so much of his early efforts went into erecting a make-shift flagpole in the hope that he would be able to attract attention. He did this by standing the water cask on one end and sticking a wooden spar through the other end, but, in his clumsiness, he spilled much of the precious water.

He very probably knew of earlier instances when sailors had been shipwrecked and then rescued from the island – and may even have known of the experiences of William Dampier and the sixty men on board *Roebuck*, stuck on the island for six weeks just a few years earlier. Dampier's exploits have been given in more detail in Chapter 6.

In the early days he caught several ground-nesting birds called boobies, which were in plentiful supply. He also encountered turtles, turning them over and cutting them up with his hatchet. But he was unable to catch up with the wild goats which he found in the interior, and his diaries show signs of self-pity and deep melancholy.

The journal shows that Leendert had some thoughts for the future, as shown by his attempt to plant seeds (pea and onions) but later entries show that the seedlings were all eaten by vermin.

Much of his time was spent high in the hills, scouring the horizon for signs of any sails. There were none, and his efforts meant that he neglected the more pressing need to establish a water supply and construct a safe shelter. He was to pay a heavy price for these omissions later on in his stay. His lack of care and attention led him to leave a burning piece of tinder cloth in his tent when he went off exploring. He returned to find that the smouldering cloth had set fire to a pile of clothing, scorching the tent and damaging his Bible. He made light of the incident with the words: 'I have lost nothing by it but a banyan shirt, a corner of my quilt, and my Bible singed.'

It soon became obvious that the lack of fresh water was going to be a major problem and by the middle of June his cask was completely empty. He resorted to digging for water, but without success. Matters eased slightly when he followed a group of goats up into the hills, and in doing so found a small trickle of water emerging from the rocks. But that too dried up in the heat of the summer and he was soon hallucinating as he became more and more dehydrated. Before long the diary is filled with entries about apparitions, evil spirits, imps and the reproachful voices of men from his recent past. He was to write:

In the night was surprised by a noise round my tent of cursing and swearing, and the most blasphemous conversations that I ever heard... My concern was so great, that I thought I should have died with the fright... anybody would have believed that the Devil had moved his quarters and was coming to keep Hell on Ascension.

On other occasions he heard voices which he thought 'belonged to an intimate acquaintance of mine; and I really thought that I was sometimes touched by an invisible spirit'.

These apparitions disturbed Leendert so much that he was scared to sleep at night without a light. Even this solace was denied him, when his fumbling knocked over and broke the saucer holding the burning wick and fat. On one occasion he failed to get back to the tent before darkness fell and was forced to spend the night in the open. ('I was obliged to lie under the open sky, and there were vast number of rats.')

Later versions of the journal contain the passage that: 'I hope this my punishment in this world may suffice for my most heinous crime of making use of my fellow creature to satisfy my lust, whom the Almighty creator had ordained another sex for.' This wording does not appear in the first version, which although full of self-pity, makes little reference to the crimes which he had committed.

As high summer developed, Leendert found himself completely deprived of water. He was desperate for moisture and resorted to eating the blood from turtles – and even spoke enthusiastically about drinking the urine from the turtle bladder. He used his own urine to try and boil up a cup of tea.

On 31 August he wrote: 'I was walking, or, more properly speaking, crawling on the sand, for I could not walk three steps together.' When he caught a small turtle, he gave this description:

I ... cut off his head with my razor, and lay all along and sucked his blood as it run out ... I got out some of its eggs, and carried them home, and fry'd them, and afterwards drank some boil'd piss mixed with tea; which, though it was so nauseous, revived me much.

By now he was become weaker by the day, writing: 'I am so much decay'd, that I am a perfect skeleton, and cannot write the particulars, my hand shakes so.' Somehow, he managed to keep up his journal, but the entries were becoming shorter and shorter. Most entries were 'ditto'; 7 October saw a brief note: 'My wood's all gone, so that I am forced to eat raw flesh and salted fowls. I cannot live long, and I hope the Lord will have mercy on my soul.' After that, the word 'ditto' is repeated over and over again, right up to the final entry on 14 October.

It was to be three months before his journal was found by the passing *James and Mary*, and it is not known whether he died immediately after the final entry, or whether he soldiered on for a few more weeks. There is no evidence as to how or where he died and realistically he may have just stumbled out into the sea and drowned, chasing imaginary sails or escaping from his devils. The 1726 version of the *Journal* has the words:

The journal ends here abruptly, whether urg'd by encreasing Despair he laid violent hands on his Life, or whether he died by Thirst, Sickness, Accident, or was delivered by some ship that might touch at any part of the Island is as yet a Mystery. FINIS.

The later editions of the *Journal* contain editorial comment about Sin, Repentance and Punishment, and they help to remind us that without the original journal, it is impossible to know how much didactic moralising has been inserted throughout the text. Stripped of the repugnance against sodomy, the journal shows a man who died because he failed to prioritise his labours – there *was* a natural source of water on the island, but he never found it. There were caves on the island, but they went unused. He had fire but failed to stockpile wood to keep it going. He was surrounded by goats but was unable to catch them. It is a reminder that survival can take a remarkable strength of character – and without it, the castaway's days are invariably numbered.

The case also shows much about eighteenth-century attitudes towards homosexuality. The public regarded it with abhorrence and would read the journal with a feeling that 'the Dutch had got it right' and knew how to punish such wrongdoers. In fact, there are numerous cases of sodomy in the eighteenth-century records of the VOC, with many of the perpetrators either being hanged or left to die. There is even one case where two men were tied up, starved on deck for five days, and then tossed overboard to drown in a weighted sack.

The story also finds echoes in the punishment meted out by pirates towards their victims. These might either be captives who refused to sign up to life as an outlaw, or one of their own number who had broken the Pirate's Code, for instance by stealing, or failing to bring looted goods into general account. Being marooned on a deserted island, or on a sandbar at low tide, was an oft-repeated punishment. Sometimes the victim was given a pistol and a single bullet, so that he had the option of committing suicide.

Some marooned pirates survived the ordeal. In 1720 the pirate Edward England was marooned on the island of Mauritius, then known as L'Ile de France, along with three loyal crew members. They were left to scavenge, without provisions, but managed to survive for four months and during that time were able to construct a small boat. They then sailed to the pirate haven of St Augustine's Bay on the island of Madagascar. There England died after a few months, possibly from a tropical disease, having lived for a while on the charity of other pirates.

Chapter 15

The Forgotten Slaves of Tromelin

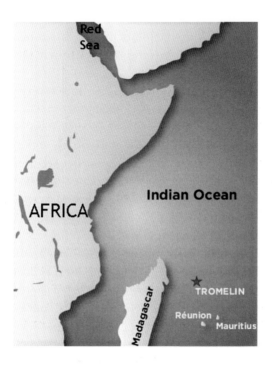

This extraordinary castaway story is in some ways the most remarkable of them all. Who could possibly imagine that it would be possible to take a group of hill-people, natives unversed in sailing or fishing, and place them on an island without a stream, without a single tree, without shelter, without edible vegetation, and without animals – and then expect any of them to be alive fifteen years later? And yet that is what happened on L'île de Sable, an island barely twenty-four inches above sea level, subject to constant inundation and in the path of the cyclones which barrel through this part of the Indian Ocean.

The island's name, L'île de Sable (the Island of Sand) reflects the fact that for centuries no one was quite sure where it was. There were stories of a low-lying island, an obvious hazard to navigation, but no one was sure whether it was close to Africa, or India, or somewhere in the middle. Sailors in the eighteenth century believed that there was a sandy spit of land somewhere in the area north of L'île de France (Mauritius). The area consists of a ring of volcanic outcrops swirling north and east from the tip of Madagascar and reveals itself as a string of volcanic islands.

L'île de Sable, now known by the name of Tromelin Island, is claimed by both France and Mauritius. The French have had a small weather centre there since 1954, but since 2010 the two countries have very sensibly agreed a shared management arrangement. Quite why anyone would want it is a bit of a mystery, because it is remarkably barren and hostile.

It is not really the most inviting of islands; the coral reef which encircles the island makes for some appallingly treacherous conditions for anyone arriving by sea. Indeed there is only one safe landing place, to the northwest of the island, where there is a narrow pass. Even at this one point, docking can only be done in calm weather. Nowadays, access to the weather station is by plane. There is a small landing strip crossing the island, enabling a monthly visit by plane, but there is precious little else on the island.

It is barren, and is covered in bits of broken coral, and has no usable vegetation or trees. It has no suitability for cultivating either crops, vegetables or fruit; 250 years ago it would have been an equally hostile environment – not a place where you would choose to stay.

What the island does have is a lot of Red-footed Boobies, Brown Boobies, White Tern, Masked Terns and Brown Noddies which nest among the scrubland. Above all, the island has Sooty Terns – tens of thousands of them. As for land-based creatures the place is over-run with hermit-crabs, which carpet the whole island. The waters around the island teem with fish, and also with turtles which come ashore on the island to lay their eggs in the coral sand, so there is certainly a food-supply, particularly if residents are cunning and determined.

That is the background to a voyage undertaken in 1761 by a small sailing vessel known as a flute. It was called *Utile* and belonged to the French East India Company. The flute followed a design made popular in Holland in the late seventeenth century and was particularly designed to carry cargo. *Utile* had originally belonged to the French Navy, but had been sold to the French East India Company and was being used to transport people and merchandise from Europe to the islands off the eastern coast of Africa.

The French East India Company had been formed in 1664 as France's answer to the Dutch East India Company and was designed to strengthen French trading interests in the area from the east coast of Africa throughout the Indian and Pacific Oceans. It had been granted an exclusive trading monopoly with Madagascar by the French king, as well as a more limited monopoly in any other areas where the company established new trade outlets.

As the fledgling company grew, it established itself in India and developed ports on L'île de Bourbon (now Réunion) and L'île de France (Mauritius) – bringing the company into direct conflict with the aspirations of the British East India Company. However, the French company suffered throughout from under-funding, and following defeats on the Indian sub-continent at the hands of Britain under the leadership of Robert Clive it faced financial ruin.

In 1769 the French King abolished the Company and took over its debts. Prior to that date the Company had appointed island governors, but after 1769 the French crown assumed direct control over appointments. In practice, the Company enjoyed one last hurrah, being reconstituted in 1785 before finally being wound up, bankrupt, in 1794.

All this was in the future when, in 1761, *Utile* left the port of Bayonne for its long voyage to the East Indies. It was due to make a stopover to re-provision in Madagascar. The intention had always been that the captain would load food in Madagascar before heading for L'île de France, where food shortages were endemic. The Captain, Jean de La Fargue, decided that he would make a bit of money on the side on the final leg of his journey (the Madagascar to L'île de France trip) by loading 160 Malagasy slaves on board, nailed inside wooden cages. The slaves had been captured and brought down to the coast from the mountainous interior. *Utile*'s captain would have known full well that the trade in slaves to L'île de France had been halted six months earlier – not for any humanitarian reason, but because there were already food shortages on the island. The governor was known to be anxious to prevent any more demands on the depleted food stocks.

Jean de La Fargue's route from Madagascar should not have taken him particularly close to the uncharted Ile de Sable, but the greedy captain decided not to go direct to L'île de France with his illicit cargo. Instead of passing close to Réunion, he headed straight for the small island of Rodrigues, passing smack through the uncharted waters where L'île de Sable lay hidden in the darkness. To make matters worse, the night of 31 July 1761 was moonless and at half past ten in the evening the Captain encountered a violent storm. *Utile* was driven on to the submerged coral reef which surrounded the island. The ship started to break in two and the logbook for *Utile* contains this dramatic report of what happened next:

The coming of day and the sight of land, which diminished our terrors, reduced none of the furies of the sea. Several people threw themselves into the water with a line to reach the land, to no end. A few reached the shore.... We had to haul some others back over the debris, where they drowned. We were terrified all the while because the shattered stern of the ship, on which we were standing, opened and closed at each moment, cutting more than one person in two.

The logbook continues:

> *Eventually the ship turned its stern towards the shore, allowing the sailors to establish a rope-way to the island. All the remaining Gentlemen and crew were saved. Our losses were only twenty white men, and two gentlemen and many blacks …*

The 'white men' would have been the crew, and the 'gentlemen' were the paying passengers. Many of the slaves who died drowned because the hatches were nailed down.

Another contemporary description stated: 'Traversing a host of dangers, most of the crew succeeded in reaching the island. Almost all were injured, maimed, and covered in bruises; they were spectres rather than men.' The logbook continues:

> *We made a big tent with the main sail and some flags and we [i.e. the gentlemen] lived there with all the supplies. The crew were placed in small tents. We started to feel very strongly the shortage of water. A number of blacks died, not being given any.*

After a couple of weeks, the 122 'gentlemen and sailors' managed to dig a small well in the crushed coral which formed the base of the island. In time this was replaced with a new well, the 'thick, white, milky liquid from the first proving to be toxic.' They also made a forge, so that they could work metal and repair their implements. It appears that there was no shortage of food, with the men slaughtering hundreds of sooty terns, as well as capturing several of the island turtles, which could weigh up to 500 kilos.

What happened next gives a fascinating picture of eighteenth-century European society. The log book goes on to explain that the slaves lived on their own at the extreme northern tip of the island, while the Europeans lived in the centre of the island, along its western coast. The Europeans had the shelter and protection of tents made from sails taken from the abandoned ship, whereas the slaves had nothing. The log book also recounted that Barthelemy Castellan, the first officer on *Utile*, had emerged as the leader of the survivors, replacing the captain who had suffered a complete physical and mental breakdown.

Castellan, who had sailed on slave ships before, was worried about the risk of violence and disorder. He urgently set about building an escape vessel, but had to contend with three significant problems: the ship's carpenter had no actual woodworking skills, and had certainly never built a boat from scratch; there were no trees on the island and therefore all wood would have to be salvaged from the wreck, much of which was submerged; and most important of all, most of the crew were disinclined to work. In fact, all but twenty preferred to go off bird-hunting rather than agreeing to manual labour.

Castellan overcame the first problem; though he had no naval-architecture training, he skilfully sketched plans for an escape vessel which he called *Providence*. That left the second problem: lack of wood. More especially, there was a shortage of timber of the right length. Castellan was looking to build a kind of raft with sides five feet high. His plan was for a craft 45 ft long, but as none of the salvaged timbers were more than 33 ft long the plans had to be scaled back, restricted in the length of beam to the longest piece of timber available. Reducing the length by 12 ft had an unfortunate consequence: it meant that the capacity for passengers was reduced by fifty per cent.

The third problem, lack of manual labour, could be overcome with the help of the Malagasy slaves. A contemporary report suggests that 'The slaves toiled with great zeal in this work'. Nothing suggests that coercion was involved, and presumably the slaves saw it as their best chance of getting off the island.

There is no record of the discussion which must have taken place, possibly right at the very last moment, in which the slaves were informed that there would be no room on board and that all of them would have to remain on the island. On 27 September 1761 the 123-strong white crew and passengers boarded their makeshift raft, christened *Providence*, and waved goodbye to the slaves. They included perhaps 100 men who had played no part in the construction of *Providence*, and yet who felt justified in taking a place on board. It was said that the French sailors boarded arm-in-arm so that they could all fit in. The dumbfounded slaves stood in utter, oppressive, silence.

The abandoned slaves were left with sufficient food and supplies to last for perhaps three months, along with a letter stating that they had behaved well. This was presumably intended to convince any passing ship's captain that they were not troublemakers and had brought no harm to their European masters. They were also given something altogether more intangible – the word of Castellan that he would come back for them. This promise was made because Castellan was convinced that the provisions which he had left behind would be sufficient to last until he had reached safety and was able to commission a vessel to come back for the stranded slaves. First though, he had to steer his crew in an open raft across 550 kilometres of open ocean, heading west towards Madagascar. The men were crammed together in conditions little better than those afforded to the slaves on their journey some six months earlier, but at least they had fresh water and basic food supplies. They enjoyed incredible fortune from favourable winds, reaching the east coast of Madagascar after just four days. Castellan had estimated a voyage of several weeks and must have been delighted that only one person on board died during the journey.

On reaching dry land the crew declared to the authorities: 'We affirm with truth that, after God, we owe our escape from that island to [Castellan] alone … we acted only to obey his counsel and orders.' The declaration mentions that Castellan had planned to go back for the slaves but added that: 'Castellan could not secure the spare sails required to do so.'

The survivors were greeted with amazement by the authorities on Madagascar, but try as he might, Castellan was unable to persuade the authorities to mount a rescue mission. The French East India Company, in charge of the island, were angry at the loss of the ship, brought about by the illegal act of the captain in taking slaves on board against Company rules. After a few weeks Castellan and his crew were ordered to go to L'île de France, the centre of French influence and power. By then, 25 November, the slaves had already been stranded for two months and must have started to despair, with food supplies running out.

It is believed that of the 160 slaves originally on the boat, seventy-two died before they were brought ashore, twenty-eight died of thirst shortly after landing, leaving sixty slaves trying to cope on their own, without basic resources. It is impossible to imagine the helplessness and anger felt by the abandoned slaves – they had, after all, contributed most of the labour required in constructing *Providence,* but at the end of the day they were treated as expendable – as cargo of very little value.

Weeks passed into months, and months into years. It is highly likely that many of the abandoned slaves would have died within a very short period of time, and there are suggestions that one group made a secondary raft, with sails made from bird feathers sewn together in sheets. If it sailed away, it was never heard of again. The remaining survivors built a raised platform as a look-out, but no one came.

Why not? Quite possibly the governor on Île de France had an ulterior motive; it is thought that he was doing a bit of slave trading on the side and did not want to see the market price of his slaves undercut by new arrivals. In addition, France was then at war with Britain and there were no ships to be spared to go on a mercy mission of this nature. And of course, there was always the argument that the mission would be a waste of time – and that the slaves must have perished already.

Castellan had given his word and was determined to stay put on the island until he had fulfilled his promise. The other crew returned to Europe, whereas Castellan took a job aboard a supply ship calling in on the local (inhabited) islands. At one stage, in January 1762, he nearly managed to persuade the captain of the supply ship to make a small detour, to see if there were signs of life on L'île de Sable, but the attempt had to be abandoned when news came through that there was a British naval vessel in the area.

A year passed, and Castellan realised that his plans were futile. He returned to France but continued to lobby the authorities for funds to mount a rescue mission. By then the French East India Company had gone into liquidation, but after a whole decade had passed the French Naval Secretary decided to accede to

Castellan's request. It was 1772, and it took a further three years before the decision was implemented. In August 1775, fourteen years after the original wreck, a rescue ship reached L'île de Sable, but heavy seas meant that a rescue attempt had to be abandoned, after a dinghy had tried to make it to the shore through the towering breakers. One of the men on board the dinghy scrambled ashore, but the other had to be hauled back to the safety of the naval vessel. The end result was one extra person on the island – the captain of the rescue ship thought that he could make out perhaps thirteen people on the island, so now there were possibly fourteen people needing to be rescued.

There was also reason for hope – those on board the ship thought that they could see smoke, as well as the outline of low-lying shelters. Suddenly there was a greater urgency to carry out a follow-up visit. Two more ships were commissioned to visit the island, but both failed to get ashore. Finally, on 29 November 1776, a vessel called *Dauphine* encountered favourable winds and calm seas and managed to put a dinghy ashore. By then the marooned islanders had been there for fifteen years.

Dauphine was under the command of Captain de Tromelin, a member of a French aristocratic family based in Nantes. In the space of that single morning the island went from being unnamed and uncharted, to being called Tromelin Island. The rescuers were met by just seven survivors – all of them women, dressed (if you can call it that) in bird feathers. There was no sign of any of the male slaves, or of the Frenchman stranded the previous year. To add to the puzzle, one of the women was holding a baby, reckoned to be about 8 months old, and looking very much paler-skinned than the other slaves.

The survivors were taken on board *Dauphine* and evacuated to Mauritius, where it became apparent that the Frenchman had led a futile attempt by three male and three female survivors to build a rescue raft out of what little wood was still available from the original wreck. They left the other women behind – but not before the Frenchman had fathered the child. Those on the raft were never seen or heard of again and must have perished on the open ocean.

When they reached L'île de France they found an island controlled not by a corrupt governor appointed by the French East India Company, but by a governor appointed directly by the French king. He asserted that the rescued women were free, because they had been caught and forced into slavery illegally. They were baptised and the mother of the child was christened 'Eve'. The boy was named 'Jacques Moses' ('Jacques' being the governor's first name, and 'Moses 'after the prophet, who was born a slave and whose name means 'drawn out of the water').

One letter survives from the time, and it records statements taken from some of the survivors. After briefly describing their daily lives, the letter states that 'Eighteen of the male survivors tried to leave the island almost immediately after they were abandoned, using a homemade raft, with sails made of bird feathers. Then several women died at different stages. This is almost all that we knew.'

It is unclear whether the slaves had managed to make fire, or whether they had succeeded in the seemingly impossible task of keeping the same fire burning for fifteen years, despite cyclones and inundations. There is no record that they knew how to make fire, or had any flints, but clearly they had been able to cook in a communal kitchen, eating mostly birds and turtles. They dressed themselves in clothes made of bird feathers, strung together with thread salvaged from *Utile*.

Having told their stories, the women disappeared from history. No one made a best-selling story of their adventure; no one suggested a play, or a pantomime, or a promotional tour of the French colonies. They simply became absorbed into the population on what became known as Mauritius.

As for the other participants in the story, Castellan died in 1782 and was may not have known that the islanders had ever been located. He was a hospital administrator at the time of his death, and there are records to show that he continued to cajole and pester the authorities until the very end of his life. As for Tromelin, he returned to France but his family lost all their estates in the revolution of 1789. He moved to Lyon, and was to die at the age of 81, in 1815. The man who was governor on L'île de France when *Utile* was wrecked, headed home for France in 1790, but died during the journey.

It is interesting to see how the remarkable story of survival came to be told. Credit must go to the French mathematician and philosopher called the Marquis de Condorcet. After the French Revolution he became a respected human rights activist. In the previous decade he had written pamphlets promoting the idea of equality – equality for women, and equality for slaves. In one of the pamphlets he mentioned the survival story on L'île de Sable, although he was muddled in his figures, stating that 300 slaves were abandoned on an island which was totally submerged every day at high tide. He went on to say: 'Seven negro women and a child born on the island were found, the men having all died, either of misery, or hopelessness, or attempting to escape.'

The French authorities took a dim view of the scorn and criticism heaped on them by de Condorcet and chucked him in prison. There he died, in mysterious circumstances, in 1794. But the pamphlets gave him a posthumous fame, and in time the National Assembly decreed that slavery was illegal, as a crime against humanity. Slavery was abolished, at least in theory, but this decision was reversed by the Emperor Napoleon in 1804. Slavery was finally abolished in the French colonies in 1848.

Back on Tromelin Island there is one reminder of the wreck of the *Utile* – her anchor still sits in full view, in the surf just off the coast. More recently, archaeological excavations have taken place and these have uncovered much about the life of the survivors. A number of stone-walled huts have been exposed with walls a metre and a half thick, constructed from coral blocks. In all probability these shelters were roofless, because there was no timber for rafters, but the narrowness of the rooms must have afforded a measure of protection, however small. The communal cooking area has been revealed, along with cooking utensils which show signs of having been repaired. Homemade rivets suggest that some pans were repaired over and over again, robbing strips of metal from other utensils, and then being held together with coils of metal, hammered firmly through holes to act as a rivet.

The one thing which has never been located is any sign of human burial. In the nineteenth century a Royal Naval ship had reported seeing a graveyard on the island, but the archaeologists were unable to find any trace of it. It is however possible that it is located immediately under the one building on the island – the French Meteorological Station. One other suggestion is that any graveyard would have been looted over the intervening years – by treasure hunters. The island is, after all, in an area where piracy was common, and is close to the eighteenth-century pirate stronghold of L'île de Marie, off the eastern coast of Madagascar.

The excavations have been headed by Frenchman Max Guérout who says:

It is clear that, left to their own devices, these slaves have taken charge and managed to recreate a society to ensure their survival. These were not people who were overwhelmed by their fate. They were people who worked together successfully in an orderly way. We have found evidence of where they lived and what they ate. It is a very human story, a story of the ingenuity and instinct for survival of people who were abandoned because they were regarded by some of their fellow human beings as less than human.

He goes on to explain that the excavations reveal four distinct phases during the fifteen-year occupation of the island, stating that this is a clear sign that the survivors adapted as they moved away from simply waiting to be rescued, towards establishing a civilisation intended to be permanent.

Following these discoveries, various documentary films have been made, in French, and a number of travelling exhibitions have taken place in France, aimed at reminding people of their heritage and of a little-known period of their history. This has perhaps helped to throw more light on the whole question of slavery in the area around India and in the Far East, instead of concentrating solely on the better-known aspects of slavery in the Caribbean.

Chapter 16

Captain Bligh and Fletcher Christian

It is easy to think that we all know the story of Captain Bligh: his name is synonymous with portrayals in films in which he is the cruel, unfeeling martinet who gets his comeuppance when the good looking, hard-done-by Fletcher Christian gives him a taste of his own medicine by casting him away in a boat. There is, of course, rather more to it than that, and the journal which Bligh kept during his remarkable voyage in an open boat, travelling with eighteen men with limited supplies of food, suggests a man who was a hugely competent sailor, a brilliant navigator, and a man who put the concerns of his men above those of his own. William Bligh was born in Plymouth in 1754 and had gone to sea  as an 8-year-old, rising through the different ranks and passing his examinations to become qualified as a lieutenant in 1776. Commissions were in short supply and a posting as lieutenant was not forthcoming immediately. However, he clearly showed considerable skill and initiative as a 22 -year-old because he was singled out by Captain James Cook to be Sailing Master of *Resolution* when she sailed on what was to be Cook's third and final voyage across the Pacific Ocean. The voyage lasted three years during which the ship explored the islands of the North Pacific, and Bligh showed his abilities as a map-maker and surveyor of the various coastlines.

Cook was killed in Hawaii by native islanders on Valentine's Day 1779 and when the *Resolution* returned to England towards the end of 1780 Bligh got married, fathered three daughters and became a captain in the merchant navy, making several journeys to the West Indies. On some of these voyages he was accompanied by Fletcher Christian, and the two became friends. Returning to the Royal Navy in 1787 Bligh was placed in charge of HMS *Bounty*, a merchant ship purchased by the navy to carry out a mission suggested by the botanist Sir Joseph Banks. He had noticed the ease with which the breadfruit tree grew throughout the Pacific and was certain that it would adapt to being introduced as a valuable source of food in the West Indies. The plantations were experiencing food shortages, especially with an increasing slave population to feed. The breadfruit could reasonably be expected to provide cheap sustenance and so *Bounty* was dispatched to collect seedlings and to take them to the Caribbean.

Bligh had a crew of forty-four, including Fletcher Christian as Master's Mate, and all went relatively smoothly as 1,015 breadfruit plants were collected and put on board. The ship left Tahiti in early April 1789 after a stay of nearly half a year – six months during which the crew had thoroughly settled in to the Tahitian lifestyle. Master's Mate Fletcher Christian had taken a Tahitian girl called Maimiti as his wife and was far from pleased to be required to leave a sybaritic life behind and to face the rigours of the Pacific Ocean. Christian also felt a burning resentment at the way he was singled out for treatment by Bligh, feeling that he was being continually victimised.

While just thirty nautical miles off the island of Tofua, now known as Tonga, Christian led a mutiny in the early morning of 28 April 1789. Bligh was forced into the *Bounty*'s longboat along with eighteen men who were unwilling to join the mutineers. It probably never crossed the minds of Christian and his supporters that Bligh might actually survive and make it back to England: they were given minimum supplies and, as an afterthought, four cutlasses presumably so that they could defend themselves if they made it to landfall on Tofua. Well aware of the fate which had befallen Captain Cook, Bligh must have been in no doubt that he was being cast away to die.

Bligh commenced writing a journal, and started it by describing how he had been set upon while he was asleep in his cabin, his hands tied and at gunpoint forced into the longboat. He also described that the others were allowed to collect specified items for their voyage: twine, canvas, lines, sails, cordage, a 28-gallon cask of water and the carpenters tool chest. He went on:

> *Mr Samuel got 150lbs. of bread with a small quantity of rum and wine. He also got a quadrant and compass for the boat; but was forbidden, on pain of death to touch either map, ephemeris, book of astronomical observations, sextant, time keeper or any of my surveys or drawings.*

Bligh described how 'a few pieces of pork' were thrown down to them, sixteen in all, each weighing 2 lb. The rum amounted to six quarts (i.e. twelve pints) and the wine ran to six bottles. Bligh continued: 'After having undergone a great deal of ridicule and been kept some time to make sport for these unfeeling wretches, we were at length cast adrift in the open ocean'.

The men rowed towards landfall, realizing that these provisions were never going to be enough to take them very far. Bligh had been on Tofua before and knew some of the leaders but when they first reached landfall they encountered nobody. Rough seas prevented them leaving their landing place, and the men survived for several days on a measure of grog and a small piece of bread. At length the landing party managed to knock down twenty coconuts and take them back on board and on another expedition the men found a few plantains. These were brought back and shared out together with a minute amount of the pork. Bligh realised from the rough terrain and poor soil that they had not landed on one of the fertile, productive, islands, writing that 'we considered ourselves on as miserable a spot of land as could well be imagined'. After a few days they came across natives, who seemed friendly and were prepared to exchange coconuts, plantains and breadfruit for a few buckles and beads. But gradually more and more natives appeared, including some who recognised Bligh from his days with Captain Cook. Their initial affability turned to hostility and, as Bligh noted: 'the beach was now lined with the natives, and we heard nothing but the knocking of stones together, which they had in each hand. I knew very well this was the sign of an attack'.

Bligh told his men to expect an attack but they were ill-armed to defend themselves as two of the four cutlasses were still on board the boat, anchored offshore. A night-time escape seemed the best option and as the sun set the men gathered their belongings and headed out into the surf. The leaders of the native group made it clear that they would be killed if they tried to leave the island, and suddenly some 200 men, armed with stones, started their attack. One of Bligh's men, John Norton, bravely ran to cast off the stern rope but was caught and stoned to death. As the natives started to haul in the rope to bring the boat back to shore, Bligh had the presence of mind to cut through the rope with his knife and they desperately tried to row away. The natives set off in pursuit in their canoes, bombarding the escapers with large stones.

They, however, could paddle round us, so that we were obliged to sustain the attack without being able to return it, except with such stones as lodged in the boat, and in this I found we were very inferior to them. We could not close, because our boat was lumbered and heavy, and that they knew very well: I therefore adopted the expedient of throwing overboard some cloaths, which they lost time in picking up; and, as it was now almost dark, they gave over the attack, and returned towards the shore, leaving us to reflect on our unhappy situation.

All those on board must have been appalled, having watched a colleague murdered in cold blood, but in a sense it united the survivors. As Bligh wrote:

We were now sailing along the west side of the island Tofoa, and my mind was employed in considering what was best to be done, when I was solicited by all hands to take them towards home: and, when I told them no hopes of relief for us remained, but what I might find at New Holland, until I came to Timor, … where was a Dutch settlement, but in what part of the island I knew not, they all agreed to live on one ounce of bread, and a quarter of a pint of water, per day. Therefore, after examining our stock of provisions, and recommending this as a sacred promise for ever to their memory, we bore away across a sea, where the navigation is but little known, in a small boat, twenty-three feet long from stern to stern, deep laden with eighteen men; without a chart, and nothing but my own recollection and general knowledge of the situation of places, assisted by a book of latitudes and longitudes, to guide us. I was happy, however, to see every one better satisfied with our situation in this particular than myself.

The sides of their heavily laden boat were barely seven inches above sea level and water was constantly being taken on board. Two men were engaged in baling out, non-stop, day and night. The lack of protection meant that when the seas got rough, Bligh had little choice but to go with the waves, since trying to steer a predetermined course would inevitably have meant hitting waves side-on, causing the vessel to capsize. It is a testament to Bligh's remarkable skills of navigation that he was able even to consider what was to be a journey of 3,500 nautical miles based entirely on his observations of winds, tides and currents, together with his rough memory of his previous visit to this area in the world.

Conditions were terrible, with gales and heavy rain keeping the men cold and soaked for days and nights on end. Even the teaspoonful of rum allocated most days can have done little to lift morale when facing near-certain death. They passed numerous small islands but Bligh knew full well that without guns they would not stand a chance against the native islanders, and so they kept out at sea. They collected rainwater, they made a makeshift shelter with canvas, they tried to keep the bread dry in the carpenter's tool-box, and they prayed. They dreaded the nights because they were so cold, and yet Bligh was able to write that he thought that the wet, cold, weather was more merciful than an overbearing heat which would have killed them from heat stroke and dehydration.

The rations had to be reduced still further as Bligh recalculated how much food they would need for the remaining journey. He remarked in his journal:

The allowance which I now regularly served to each person was one 25th of a pound of bread, and a quarter of a pint of water, at sun-set, eight in the morning, and at noon. To-day I gave about half an ounce of pork for dinner, which, though any moderate person would have considered but a mouthful, was divided into three or four.

On 24 May, Bligh made a journal entry that they caught a bird, called a noddy. It was about the size of a pigeon, and it was duly killed, plucked and divided up into eighteen tiny pieces. In order to ensure a fair distribution of the pieces, which still included the beak and all the bones, one man turned his back on the others and had to answer the question put to him: 'who shall have this piece?' In this way the 'treat' was allocated without favour, and it became a method of distribution used on a number of occasions when they were fortunate enough to catch either noddies or boobies, described by Bligh as being the size of a small duck.

By now all the men were suffering from constant stomach pains together with cramp from lack of exercise in their lower limbs. At the end of May they encountered the crashing waves which marked the edge of the Great Barrier Reef. Crossing these breakers led them into calmer waters and eventually they decided to make landfall and to send out search parties looking for fresh food. They returned, as Bligh put it,

highly rejoiced at having found plenty of oysters and fresh water. I also had made a fire, by help of a small magnifying glass, that I always carried about me, to read off the divisions of my sextants; and, what was still more fortunate, among the few things which had been thrown into the boat and saved, was a piece of brimstone and a tinder-box, so that I secured fire for the future.

Some of the men gorged themselves on berries which they found, despite the fear of poisoning, and became violently sick. Bligh noticed that one particular berry was eaten by the indigenous birds and therefore reasoned that those berries were safe to eat. He was right. After a few days collecting oysters and fresh water, the men could see that they had been spotted by natives; it was time to go and find another place to re-provision. By now some of Bligh's men were getting fractious and Bligh records one instance when his authority was challenged and he had to pick up a cutlass and threaten the man before things quietened down. On another, he gave one of the men a good beating for having gone off on his own and caught nine noddies, which he killed and ate without sharing with the others.

Bligh continued to sail a north-westerly course, up the inside of the Barrier Reef, before reaching the open ocean and heading in the direction of Timor. The men were deteriorating rapidly with two in particular near death. Bligh records the extra care given to these two:

I could only assist them by a tea-spoonful or two of wine, which I had carefully saved, expecting such a melancholy necessity. Among most of the others I observed more than a common inclination to sleep, which seemed to indicate that nature was almost exhausted.

He seemed to pride himself in making sure that his own suffering was at least as great as the men who served him, writing:

For my own part, a great share of spirits, with the hopes of being able to accomplish the voyage, seemed to be my principal support; but the boatswain very innocently told me, that he really thought I looked worse than any one in the boat. The simplicity with which he uttered such an opinion diverted me, and I had good humour enough to return him a better compliment.

Days turned into weeks with the same boring monotony: baling, trying to get dry, eking out the meagre supplies, keeping up morale. Finally, on 12 June, they reached part of the island of Timor and Bligh was able to write:

It is not possible for me to describe the pleasure which the blessing of the sight of land diffused among us. It appeared scarce credible, that in an open boat, and so poorly provided, we should have been able to reach the coast of Timor in forty-one days after leaving Tofoa, having in that time run, by our log, a distance of 3618 miles.

He still had no idea where the Dutch settlement was based, but when the bosun and the gunner went ashore they returned with news that they had come across some friendly islanders. These gave the men a small quantity of turtle meat and Indian corn. Bligh wanted to get to the Dutch settlement and needed one of the islanders to come as a pilot, or as he put it:

From these people I learned, that the governor resided at a place called Coupang, which was some distance to the N E. I made signs for one of them to go in the boat, and show me Coupang, intimating that I would pay him for his trouble; the man readily complied, and came into the boat.

Off they sailed, this time with a double portion of bread and a little wine being given to each person, reaching 'Coupang' on 14 June. To their amazement they came across an English sailor and were quickly provided with food and brought to meet the governor. As Bligh described it, they were like spectres:

> *Our bodies were nothing but skin and bones, our limbs were full of sores, and we were cloathed in rags; in this condition, with the tears of joy and gratitude flowing down our cheeks, the people of Timor beheld us with a mixture of horror, surprise, and pity.*

He had this to say about the problems of leadership:

> *In times of difficulty there will generally arise circumstances that bear more particularly hard on a commander. In our late situation, it was not the least of my distresses, to be constantly assailed with the melancholy demands of my people for an increase of allowance, which it grieved me to refuse. The necessity of observing the most rigid œconomy [sic] in the distribution of our provisions was so evident, that I resisted their solicitations, and never deviated from the agreement we made at setting out. The consequence of this care was, that at our arrival we had still remaining sufficient for eleven days, at our scanty allowance: and if we had been so unfortunate as to have missed the Dutch settlement at Timor, we could have proceeded to Java, where I was certain every supply we wanted could be procured.*

With local assistance Bligh was able to purchase 'a small schooner; 34 feet long, for which I gave 1000 rix-dollars, and fitted her for sea, under the name of His Majesty's schooner Resource.' They then set sail for Batavia, but not before one of the men, David Nelson, had succumbed to 'an inflammatory illness' and died.

The survivors reached Batavia on 1 October and Bligh was immediately struck down with fever. He recovered sufficiently, after staying a few days in the interior, to leave the island on a packet ship which left Batavia, bound for the Cape, on 16 October. That leg of the voyage took two months, and the journal ends with the words: 'On the 2nd of January, 1790, we sailed for Europe, and on the 14th of March, I was landed at Portsmouth by an Isle of Wight boat. FINIS.'

What this epic story of survival showed is that Bligh was no one-dimensional villain. He was a compassionate leader who knew that without discipline they had no chance of survival – and he was sufficiently good at explaining his motives to his men for them to accept his leadership without serious issue. It is ironic that later portrayals in books and films show him in such a bad light. His record in disciplining men, before the mutiny, shows that if anything he was rather less prone to ordering floggings and similar punishments than other naval captains. It was a harsh life, and whereas Bligh had a razor-sharp tongue and a short temper he appears to have saved this for officers whom he thought were in dereliction of their duties, rather than blaming the ordinary seamen.

Bligh was to return to the Pacific and in the years 1791–93 succeeded in bringing breadfruit to the West Indies. He led a somewhat chequered career in the navy, suffering the indignity of another mutiny in 1797 when men under his command took part in what was termed the Nore Mutiny, occasioned, it was said, by 'issues of pay and involuntary service for common seamen'. In other words, the mutiny was not particularly directed against Bligh and involved a number of ships. It was during this time that he learned that his general nickname was 'that Bounty bastard'.

He was admonished for inappropriate use of language in a court martial case brought in 1805, and later that year left for New South Wales to take up the post of governor. It was to prove to be a poisoned chalice of an appointment, with the community riven by factions and civil unrest. He was deposed and returned to England in 1810. By virtue of his long naval career (i.e. not in recognition of any particular expertise) he was made up to rear admiral in 1811 and vice admiral three years later. He died on 7 December 1817 at the age of 63, twenty-eight years after the mutiny which so nearly killed him.

The story has been the subject of numerous films; in 1916 his part was played by George Cross; in the 1933 remake entitled *In the Wake of the Bounty* he was portrayed by Mayne Lynton. More famously, Charles Laughton played the part of Bligh (albeit as a much older man) in the 1935 *Mutiny on the Bounty*, with Clark Gable starring as Fletcher Christian. Trevor Howard appeared as Bligh in the film of the same title in 1962, opposite Marlon Brando. His part was played by Anthony Hopkins in the 1984 film *The Bounty*, playing opposite Mel Gibson as Fletcher Christian.

Bligh's story of being cast away and of his subsequent rescue was not of course the end of the matter. There was also the question of what happened to the mutineers. Following Bligh's return to England, the Admiralty sent Captain Edwards on board *Pandora* on a mission to recover the mutineers and bring them back to face trial. He arrived at Tahiti in March 1791 and located fourteen of the group which had settled on Tahiti (as opposed to the ones who left with Fletcher Christian to settle on Pitcairn Island). They were rounded up and imprisoned in a wooden cage which had been placed on the deck of *Pandora* and which was, not surprisingly, nicknamed 'Pandora's Box'. However, the ship foundered on the Great Barrier Reef, with the loss of thirty-one of her crew and four of the mutineers. The remaining ten prisoners, along with the surviving crew, were transferred to open longboats where they endured a voyage very similar to that of Bligh a few years earlier, making their way up the eastern coast of New Holland (i.e. Australia) past New Guinea and over to Kupang in Timor. From there they were brought back to England and at their various trials four were acquitted. Of the six found guilty, three were pardoned. The remaining three were hanged on board HMS *Brunswick* at Portsmouth harbour on 29 October 1792.

What of Fletcher Christian? The story has been told many times; the group of mutineers split into two groups and the smaller one of nine mutineers, together with six Tahitian men and eleven Tahitian women, sailed eastward until they landed on Pitcairn Island. The Tahitians on board had actually been kidnapped when HMS *Bounty* set sail. On arrival at Pitcairn Island HMS *Bounty* was set on fire – literally a case of 'burning their boat' – and the stranded survivors had to adjust to life without modern conveniences.

Nineteen years passed before an American seal-hunting ship *Topaz* called at Pitcairn. By the time *Topaz* arrived, in 1808, all but one of the mutineers had died, the only survivor being John Adams. Nine of the eleven Tahitian women were still alive, along with a number of their children, but not one of the Tahitian males. It appears that over the years many fights had broken out between the mutineers and the Tahitian men, who were in effect being kept as slaves. There was a series of tit-for-tat murders. Infighting between the mutineers also led to loss of life. Adams changed his story on several occasions, in one instance claiming that Fletcher Christian died of natural causes and on another that he had committed suicide. One version of events has it that he went insane and threw himself off the cliffs. However, in all likelihood he was murdered in a fight with two or more of the Tahitian men, probably in 1793. They in turn were murdered by the Tahitian women. All that is certain is that Fletcher Christian was survived by his wife Maimiti and their three children: Thursday, Charles, and Mary Ann.

However, some people maintain that Fletcher Christian left the island and somehow managed to get back to England, where he was allegedly spotted in Plymouth by Peter Heywood, one of his co-mutineers. Indeed, the conspiracy theories have been around since at least 1831 when Sir John Barrow, a friend of Heywood and Second Secretary to the Admiralty, wrote:

About the years 1808 and 1809, a very general opinion was prevalent in the neighbourhood of the lakes of Cumberland and Westmoreland, that Christian was in that part of the country, and made frequent private visits to an aunt who was living there.

No one has satisfactorily explained how or when Fletcher Christian could possibly have escaped, and it remains as an example of how there is a tendency for all castaway stories to get embellished, fabricated and reinvented.

Chapter 17

Charles Barnard

Some of the castaway stories already mentioned involved comparatively warm and pleasant environments. By contrast, consider the story of betrayal, incredible hardship and injustice which marked the voyage of New Yorker Charles Barnard, just one hundred years after the voyage of Alexander Selkirk. His experience makes Selkirk's experience seem like a complete doddle. And yet, hardly anyone knows the man's name, or the appalling way he was treated.

His fate was not to be left on a pleasant island with a near tropical climate, swaying trees, fresh water and good shelter. In contrast Barnard had to endure the harsh climate of the Falkland Islands, where there were no trees to build huts, no firewood and little except penguins and seals for company.

Between 1806 and 1820 the Falklands had no permanent settlements, but they were a mecca for whalers and sea hunters. Captain Barnard was 31 years old when he took command of a schooner called *Nanina*, sailing from America in 1812. Barnard joined what was called the Great Fur Rush – a stampede of sailors heading down to the Falklands where they would spend the spring hunting seals, collecting bird eggs to eat and otherwise living off the geese and pigs released in previous years by early explorers. War with Britain had just broken out, and Barnard was keen to get under sail and start seal hunting before the ship's owners called him back to port, afraid of the risk of the ship being seized as a prize of war.

It is a mistake to think of the Falklands as being just the two main islands, East and West Falkland, and although these two account for over ninety per cent of the land mass, there are in fact over 700 islands and small islets. Barnard had divided his crew up into separate groups, each one living on a different islet, off the southern tip of East Falkland, with evocative names such as Barren Island, Bleaker Island, Bull Point and Sea Lion Island. These shore bases were served by a rowing boat christened *Young Nanina*, which would travel from one group to another, collecting the skins and replenishing food supplies. Men from the mother ship, the *Nanina*, would go ashore and hunt the pigs and geese which had been let loose on the island, and then distribute food among the seal hunters.

The seal hunting was going well, and each group had collected several hundred seal pelts. Larger seals, including the massive elephant seals, were caught and rendered down for their blubber using huge 'trying vats'. Then in early April 1813 *Nanina* was surprised to see smoke coming from one of the other islands and as they approached they could see that a number of men, and women, were waving to attract attention. Inspection revealed that there were in fact some forty-two people who had been shipwrecked. They had come from the ship *Isabella*, British registered, which was on its way back from Australia when it had been driven on to a rocky ledge just off the coast. The passengers were a motley lot – convicts who had served their time as deportees, and prostitutes who had decided to return to their home country. The captain of *Isabella* was a drunk, and apart from a couple of marines on board, discipline was almost non-existent.

Barnard brought *Nanina* alongside and discovered that those who had been shipwrecked had been stranded for several weeks. Aware that their boat was breaking up they had tried to strip it of anything that could be salvaged – timbers, rope, nails and so on, and had started to construct rudimentary shelters on the barren land. They were aware that winter was approaching and that it was unlikely that they would be given any chance of rescue until the following spring. What they did not know was that Britain was at war with America.

Those who had been shipwrecked, particularly the women, some of them with young babies, begged Barnard to end his hunt for seals and to cut short his voyage and to return to America. Barnard agreed to their request, on humanitarian grounds, because he could see that the lack of leadership or survival skills meant that the entire group was unlikely to survive. However, before agreeing to help, he asked the British to sign an agreement that they would act as if their two countries were at peace and would do nothing to damage or seize *Nanina*. This was readily agreed to – and Barnard was unwise enough to believe their assurances.

Barnard knew that they would need more supplies to feed the extra forty-two mouths on the return journey, so he enlisted the support of three of the British crew to help him, as well as an American sailor, and they set off in *Young Nanina* to hunt for extra supplies of pork, geese, and so on. Off Barnard went with his four crew chasing pigs, only to return a few days later to discover that the entire party of British castaways had disappeared, having stolen *Nanina*.

Barnard could not believe that he could have been treated in such an underhanded and devious way by the people he was prepared to help; he rowed up and down the channels which separated the various islets trying to see if the *Nanina* had simply moved to a safer anchorage. No such luck. Indeed, one of the three Britons who had accompanied him on his hunting expedition broke down in tears when he realised that he had been left behind and confessed that he knew all along that the British intended to steal *Nanina*.

Once Barnard was reconciled to the fact that he was stranded, and unlikely to find any chance of rescue for at least six months, he took stock of the situation; he had four associates, three of whom were enemies of America. Even worse, one of them, a man called Samuel Ansell, was openly hostile and violent. The other two Britons were clearly scared by Samuel Ansell and tended to do whatever he told them. That left the one American, a man who had been born a slave, but who had gone to sea once he gained his freedom.

They had the longboat *Young Nanina*, which was fine for rowing round between the islands in calm weather, but certainly not safe for crossing the open ocean, or indeed for local trips in stormy weather. Barnard ordered the men to row across to a larger island, where they hauled the boat up out of the water and turned it over onto its top so that the men could huddle under the hull, out of the wind and rain. By morning they woke to find eight inches of snow on the ground. Their fresh water had been used up, along with their limited supplies of fresh pork, which they had cooked over a small wood fire inside the boat. It is not difficult to imagine just how smoky that must have been, cooking pork inside the boat where all four men were trying to live.

Barnard refused to abandon hope; starvation and thirst were real problems but he discovered a small frozen lake of fresh water and managed to kill a couple of elephant seal cubs. Their blubber was used to keep the fire burning, but the flesh soon turned rancid. They managed to catch a couple of skuas – scavenging seabirds which competed with them for scraps, but the flesh was almost impossible to eat. The men even resorted to trying to eat the tussock grass but found that it made them sick and extremely giddy.

It was the ship's dog called *Cent* which came to their rescue, helping them to catch a small seal, two geese and a couple of foxes. The latter proved to be almost inedible and Barnard wrote, 'I ate some of their flesh but it is so very strong that nothing but the sauce of extreme hunger could force it down.'

Not for nothing did the men call their habitation 'Pinch-gut Camp'. Barnard's refusal to despair clearly inspired the party, but as days drew into weeks it became apparent that Ansell was undermining morale. He was a 26-year-old illiterate bully and a coward – and he was proving to be very difficult to control.

Barnard decided that the group should use the boat to row to a place called New Island, some miles to the west. There he set about building a stone structure as a shelter. Walls 3 ft thick were no problem to build, as there was a plentiful supply of rocks, but a total lack of timber for the roof was likely to be a problem. Fate intervened in the shape of the carcass of a whale washed up on the beach. The ribs were used as rafters, and then covered with tussock grass as a form of thatch.

Barnard assigned duties: one person was to stand on watch in case a passing ship appeared; two were to spend the day hunting with the dog; and two were to devote their time to cleaning seal skins and cutting and sewing them to make serviceable garments. By then their clothes were in shreds, and a sealskin suit was extremely welcome. Other skins were used to fashion blankets, hats and even shoes, using threads taken from a piece of old canvas mainsail. In time they managed to fill sealskin bags with discarded bird feathers, to provide pillows and quilts.

They caught wild pigs and ate shellfish and fashioned snares which caught wild geese. But, as the winter started to relax its grip, their camp became overrun with black rats. The infestation was so bad that the rats ate the food as quickly as the men could catch it. Barnard's remedy? He tied three oars together to make a pyramid and hung the food from the top. He then greased the poles with blubber so that the rats were unable to climb up and get to the food.

Spring arrived and, with it, tens of thousands of penguins and literally millions of sea birds. Suddenly there were eggs everywhere – and the five were dining off scrambled eggs, fried eggs and omelettes using eggs from penguins, geese, albatross and many other birds. It looked as if, under Barnard's inspirational leadership, the party would survive.

Then one day in October something happened to shatter Barnard's world. He had left the main camp to search for elephant seals. On returning to camp he could see his four companions rowing off into the distance. Goaded on by Samuel Ansell, the four had decided to take their chances and to leave Barnard alone and without obvious resources. He had just one knife – and a wooden club. He had no means of starting a fire, but what he did have was incredible resilience and strength of mind.

He knew that it was hopeless to think that the four would ever come back. Clearly, they intended him to die and had left him to his fate.

Desperately he managed to reignite the fire, using clumps of tussock grass. But he reasoned that if he could lift clumps of peaty soil from the top of the banks of the marshy pond, and dry out the clumps, he could burn the peat as fuel. And so it proved to be. It proved to be a highly efficient way of cooking, of keeping warm, and of keeping the fire going for hours on end.

He fashioned writing materials out of charcoal and vegetable juices, using a goose quill as a pen, enabling him to write a journal on the skins of seals which had been cleaned by scraping with the knife. Fortuitously he found a rusted saucepan lid on the shoreline, and was able to use it to cook eggs.

But it was one thing to cope physically, another to cope with the appalling loneliness and despair. Melancholy set in and he spent hours just sitting and staring at the ocean. The landscape was stark and barren, and the sea was totally devoid of sails. Months passed, until he was amazed to see *Young Nanina* containing the four men who had abandoned him come around the corner. The men were extremely surprised to find him alive – let alone sitting in front of a peat fire, cooking eggs.

Their own experience had been far more severe. Under Ansell's leadership they had gone to the site where the *Isabella* was shipwrecked, intending to strip her of anything which would be of use. All they found were some old newspapers and a few nails and screws. And Ansell was no leader. He got more and more violent towards his fellow crew members as it became apparent that they were all worse off than they had been with Barnard.

Reluctantly he had been forced to agree to go back to Barnard, and it is hard to imagine what must have been going through Barnard's mind when he realised that they wanted to come ashore. Astonishingly, he forgave them and made them welcome and indicated that he had no wish ever to mention the events of the past few months. As far as he was concerned, it was in the past and they now had to work together.

At first, all seemed fine, but at Christmas one of the four, the American former slave, confided in Barnard that Ansell was up to his old tricks and was planning to take over again. At that stage Barnard had no way of knowing how the two other British sailors would react. Would they be cowered by Ansell and follow him, or would they remain loyal to Barnard?

On 28 December the three came up to Barnard, while Ansell was absent, and pleaded with Barnard to cast Ansell adrift. He was, they said, in 'a sulky, malicious mood, planning some scheme of revenge', and they were positive that he would attempt something serious very shortly.

Within four days the entire group set off in the rowing boat for nearby Swan Island, on the pretext of hunting for seals. Once there, Ansell was dispatched to look for firewood, whereupon the rest of the party abandoned him to his solitary fate and rowed away. Barnard then ordered the remaining three men to head back to the *Isabella* to make a more thorough search for items which they could use for their survival and rescue, while he stayed behind on New Island, hunting pigs with his dog Cent, with whom he was now reunited.

The men returned from *Isabella* on 26 January and the group then decided to call in on Ansell to see how he was coping with having a dose of his own medicine. Ansell had not coped at all. In a month he had lost a huge amount of weight, was a completely broken man, and begged forgiveness. The bully had learned his lesson, and to Barnard's great credit he persuaded the other three men to agree to take Ansell back on board. They returned together to New Island, and built a new stone structure, which turned out to be windproof and watertight.

Once more, the decision was made to try and revisit the wreck of *Isabella* to look for new supplies, but this time winter was closing in and the party knew that it might be very difficult to get back from such a hazardous journey across open seas. In the end Barnard stayed behind, with Ansell, and much to the surprise of both men, a kind of fellowship developed between them. Ansell fashioned a flute and played tunes on it, while Barnard taught Ansell to read, using the few scraps of newspaper which had been salvaged from *Isabella*.

It was many weeks before the rest of the group returned, having faced mountainous seas and gale-force winds, day after day; on 6 October they managed to return, bringing with them valuable items such as rope, nails, planks and canvas.

Then finally, some eighteen months after they had been betrayed and abandoned by the British captain of *Isabella*, the group were rescued. One day in November the castaways looked out across the bay and were astonished to see two British whalers, *Asp* and *Indispensible*, moored in the harbour. The five raced down to their boat and rowed out to the ships at anchor. The first the master of *Indispensible* knew about it was when the five men clambered aboard his ship, looking like men from another planet.

As the captain later wrote he was 'confronted by a being who had more the appearance of a savage than the native of an enlightened and Christian country'. A thick beard eight inches long hung down his chest and he was attired in seal skins. The rescuers must have been astonished at the story the men regaled them with, and they soon agreed to allow the castaways to remain on board.

But the return journey was far from direct – *Indispensible* rounded the Cape and headed north for the west coast of Peru. Barnard disembarked at Lima and caught a lift on *Eliza*, a British whaler. Once he reached Más a Tierra, the island where Alexander Selkirk had been shipwrecked, Barnard asked to be dropped off. Along with another American sailor he was desperate to try and collect enough seal skins to offset the disastrous cost of the voyage. The seal hunt was only partially successful. Barnard hitched a lift with a number of vessels, ending up back at Martha's Vineyard in October 1816, some four years and four months after he had set off.

On his return he learned that the perfidious British Government had declared his original ship *Nanina* a prize of war. She had accordingly been sold, without any compensation being paid to Barnard, and with the proceeds due to go to the man who had stolen the ship from him in the first place.

In 1829 Barnard published his memoirs under the title of *A Narrative of the Sufferings and Adventures of Captain Charles H Barnard*, and that was almost the last anyone heard of him. He is understood to have returned to seal-hunting duties on the Falklands some time in 1831, but he then disappeared from view and there is no record of his subsequent life – or death. His experience showed an indomitable spirit and impressive leadership skills when faced with incredible hardship and appalling lack of support. He has been called 'the American Crusoe', but even that does not really do justice to a remarkable and tenacious survivor.

Chapter 18

Conclusion

The Age of Sail is generally used to describe the period from 1571 to 1862; it is of course a huge period and trying to describe more than a smattering of incidents involving shipwrecks and castaways is clearly impossible. Suffice to say that throughout the period there were maritime disasters, some attributable to the weather, some to faulty charts, some to human error and some to the fact that the world was still being explored and large areas were unmapped. The losses, in terms of human life, were enormous and in many cases the names of the individuals lost at sea were never recorded.

Being cast away was something which happened comparatively frequently. If the person cast away was on one of the main trade routes, the chances are that he would be picked up sooner rather than later. But for those off the beaten track it could be a long wait. For some, being cast away was a punishment, for instance at the hands of pirates. For others it was a matter of personal choice, as with Alexander Selkirk. Others were wrecked on far-off lands, and some were the victims of mutiny, as with Captain Bligh.

Those that survived did so because they were disciplined – in the case of a solo castaway, because they were self-disciplined. For many castaways, the same pattern of despair was followed by a realisation that their fate lay in their own hands; that only they could make survival possible. Give up, or fail to plan, and you were as good as lost. But for those castaways who persevered, built their shelters, parcelled out their precious resources, found a supply of fresh water and adapted to a civilisation very different to the one they were used to, there was no reason why they could not just survive, but triumph in the face of adversity. The survival of seven women, abandoned for fifteen years on Tromelin Island, is perhaps the most remarkable story of survival of them all. But for sheer, dogged, bloody-minded refusal to give up, the story of Charles Barnard takes some beating. The people who kept journals are the best remembered, but for everyone mentioned in this book there will have been another dozen who died without a trace, their hardship unknown and unacknowledged.

Nowadays, with GPS and the prevalence of mobile phones, the risk of being completely lost for more than a few days is becoming less likely, but it can still happen. We still have tales of Mexican sailors adrift in the Pacific for months on end, or of lone yachtsmen getting lost at sea. Less than 100 years ago it is thought that the pilot and explorer Amelia Earhart may have survived for a period of time after crash-landing her plane near Howland Island in the Central Pacific. And, as mankind explores space, there will no doubt be other cases where people are forced to confront the loneliness and the despair of being cut off from civilisation, forced to cope and to offer the fervent prayers for survival so eloquently described by Daniel Defoe 300 years ago.

Bibliography

Anonymous: *A wonderful history of all the storms, hurricanes, earthquakes etc...* London, 1704. Available in electronic format via Google books.

Ashton, Philip: *History of the Strange Adventures and Signal Deliverances of Mr. Philip Ashton.* Boston, 1725.

Barnard, Charles: *A Narrative of the Sufferings and Adventures of Captain Charles H Barnard in a Recent Voyage Round the World.* J.P. Callender, 1836. (reprinted in 1972 and available as a free e-Book).

Barrow, John: *The Eventful History of the Mutiny and Piratical Seizure of HMS Bounty.* Oxford University Press, London, 1831. Available online via Project Gutenberg.

Bligh, William: *A Narrative Of The Mutiny On Board His Majesty's Ship Bounty; And The Subsequent Voyage of Part of the Crew in the Ship's Boat.* London, 1790. Available online via Project Gutenberg.

Boot, Tony: *Admiralty Salvage in Peace and War 1906 – 2006: Grope, Grub and Tremble.* Pen & Sword Maritime, 2007

Brayne, Martin: *The Greatest storm: Britain's night of destruction, November 1703.* Sutton Publishing, Stroud, 2002.

Dampier, William: *A New Voyage Round the World.* London, 1697. Available in electronic format online.

Dampier, William: *A Voyage to New Holland.* London, 1703. Available in electronic format online.

Dampier, William: *A continuation of a voyage to New Holland.* Printed by W. Botham for James Knapton, London, 1709. Available in electronic format online.

Dash, Mike: *Batavia's Graveyard: The True Story of the Mad Heretic Who Led History's Bloodiest Mutiny.* Weidenfeld & Nicolson, 2002.

Defoe, Daniel: *The storm: or, a collection of the most remarkable casualties and disasters which happen'd in the late dreadful tempest by both sea and land.* London, 1704.

Defoe, Daniel: *Robinson Crusoe.* W Taylor, London, 1719. Available via Project Gutenberg at http://www.gutenberg.org/ebooks/12623

Defoe, Daniel: *The Farther Adventures of Robinson Crusoe.* W Taylor, London, 1719. Available via Project Gutenberg at http://www.gutenberg.org/ebooks/561

Defoe, Daniel: *Serious Reflections During the Life and Surprising Adventures of Robinson Crusoe.* W Taylor, London, 1720. Available online as a pdf through RCI at Rutgers.

Flemming, Gregory: *At the Point of a Cutlass: The Pirate Capture, Bold Escape, and Lonely Exile of Philip Ashton*. ForeEdge, 2014.

Frank, Katherine: *Crusoe, Daniel Defoe, Robert Knox and the creation of a myth*. The Bodley Head, London, 2011.

Gilly, W. O. S.: *Narratives of Shipwrecks of the Royal Navy; between 1793 and 1849.* (1850). Available via Project Gutenberg

Hasenbosch, L: *Sodomy punish'd: Being a true and exact relation of what befel to one Leondert Hussenlosch….* John Loveday, London 1726. (Facsimile copy available online at http://www.manfamily.org/PDFs/Sodomy%20punished%20being%20a%20true%20and%20exact.pdf).

John, Howell: *The Life and Times of Alexander Selkirk – the real Robinson Crusoe*. M Day & Co, New York, 1835.

Inglefield, John Nicholson: *Narrative, concerning the loss of His Majesty's ship, the Centaur, of seventy-four guns : and the miraculous preservation of the Pinnace, with the captain, master, and ten of the crew, in a traverse of near 300 leagues on the great western ocean, with the names of the people saved*. London, 1783.

Kingsley, Sean: *Oceans Odyssey: Deep-Sea Shipwrecks in the English Channel, the Straits of Gibraltar and the Atlantic Ocean*. Oxbow Books, Oxford, 2010.

Knox, Robert: *An Historical Relation of the Island of Ceylon in the East Indies*. London 1681

Kraske, Robert: *Marooned; the Strange but True Adventure of Alexander Selkirk, the real Robinson Crusoe*. Clarion Books, 2005.

Leys, Simon: *The Wreck of the Batavia: A True Story*. Thunder's Mouth Press, New York, 2006.

May W.E.: *The Last Voyage of Sir Clowdisley Shovel*. Journal of Navigation, XIII (1960), pp. 324-332

Navy: *A new list of all the ships and vessels of His Majesties Royal Navy.* 1710, London. Available as a facsimile copy online at https://books.google.nl/books?id=Rz0IAAAAQAAJ&pg=PT10&hl=nl&source=gbs_toc_r&cad=2#v=onepage&q&f=false

Neely, Wayne: *The Great Hurricane of 1780: The Story of the Greatest and Deadliest Hurricane of the Caribbean and the Americas*. iUniverse, Bloomington, 2012.

Pitman, Henry: *A relation of the great sufferings and strange adventures of Henry Pitman*. J Taylor, London, 1689 (also available as a free e-Book on Google as part of *Stuart Tracts 1603 – 1693* by C H Firth).

Reclus, Onésime: *Géographie de la France et de ses colonies*, Paris, 1873.

Ritsema, Alex: *A Dutch Castaway on Ascension Island in 1725*. Deventer, Netherlands, 2010.

Sabatini, Rafael: *Captain Blood*. Houghton Miffin Co. London 1922.

Schwartz, Stuart B.: *Sea of Storms*: A *History of Hurricanes in the Greater Caribbean from Columbus to Katrina*. Princeton University Press, 2015 (also available as an e-book).

Severin, Tim: *Seeking Robinson Crusoe*. Macmillan, London, 2002. Available in digitised form at https://archive.org/details/lifeadventuresof00howe

Smith, Peter C.: *Sailors on the Rocks: Famous Royal Navy Shipwrecks*. Pen & Sword Maritime, Barnsley, 2015.

I am also grateful to a number of online sites including:

'It's behind you' (giving details of pantomimes featuring Robinson Crusoe) at http://www.its-behind-you.com/storyrobinsoncrusoe.html

Internet Movie Database (giving details of the numerous Crusoe films and TV series) at http://www.imdb.com/list/ls033635772/

Captain Blood – the history behind the novel, by Cindy Vallar at http://www.cindyvallar.com/captainbloodhistory.html

Article by Dr Colin Depradine, the Principal of the Caribbean Institute for Meteorology and Hydrology (originally published in 'The Advisory', the 35th Anniversary Edition of the CIMH, 2002.)

The Dawlish Chronicles for information about the loss of the Royal George and of the Queen Charlotte http://dawlishchronicles.blogspot.co.uk/

The Maritime Archaeology Sea Trust, for the complete Royal Navy loss list http://www.thisismast.org/assets/downloads/rn-loss-list-2017-10-29.pdf

The Royal Museums Greenwich blog (particularly with reference to the measurement of longitude). See https://www.rmg.co.uk/discover/behind-the-scenes/blog

The Pipeline, specialising in stories about archaeology and heritage as news and current affairs (including information on the recovery of HMS Victory): http://thepipeline.info/blog

Image Accreditation

Text Images

Page 1 Image 1 - *Footprint in the Sand*, by Marty.

Page 2 Image 2 - *Daniel Defoe in the pillory*, line engraving by M. van der Gucht, 1706. (Wellcome Library, London)

Page 9 Image 3 - *Robinson Crusoe*, engraving by B Picart, 1720. (Rijkmuseum)

Page 15 Image 4 - *Robinson Crusoe and his pets*, Currier & Ives, New York 1874. (Library of Congress)

Page 16 Image 5 - Memorial to Alexander Selkirk, 1900. (Library of Congress)

Page 24 Image 6 - Islands off the Venezuelan coast, from Map of the West Indies by Emanuel Bowen, London, 1752. (In public domain)

Page 31 Image 7 - Map of Ceylon, 1690. (In public domain)

Page 38 Image 8 - *William Dampier in a canoe with outrigger*, off the Nicobar Islands. (Rijkmuseum)

Page 49 Image 9 - *Shipwreck of the Duke of York en route to Edinburgh*, 1683. By Caspar Luyken, 1698. (Rijkmuseum)

Page 52 Image 10 - Winstanley's Eddystone lighthouse. (In public domain)

Page 61 Image 11 - HMS *Association* sinking off the Scillies. (In public domain)

Page 68 Image 12 - *The Sinking of HMS* Victory, by Peter Monamey. (National Maritime Museum, in public domain)

Page 74 Image 13 - Satellite image of Hurricane Frances, 2004. (Courtesy of National Oceanic and Atmospheric Administration, Center for Weather and Climate)

Page 82 Image 14 - *The Sinking of HMS* Royal George *at Spithead, 1782*. (In public domain)

Page 89 Image 15 - Diary entry of Richard Hall recording the loss of Queen Charlotte.

Page 91 Image 16 - *Death Turns Pilot*, by Thomas Rowlandson 1814. (Yale Center for British Art)

Page 92 Image 17 - *Fighting on an Island after a Shipwreck (Batavia)*. Engraving, 1648. (Library of Congress)

Page 104 Image 18 - *Paper Cut Out of Three Ships Under Sail*, Richard Hall, 1780. (Author's collection)

Page 110 Image 19 - Extract from the Ortelius map of the world dated 1570, showing Ascension Island in the centre. (In public domain)

Page 116 Image 20 - Map showing Tromelin Island. (Courtesy of *Archaeology Magazine*)

Page 125 Image 21 - *Breadfruit Tree*, by Hans Hillewaert. (Creative Commons 3.0)

Page 134 Image 22 - *Storm Over a Coast*, by Giles F Phillips (1780 – 1867). (Yale Center for British Art, Paul Mellon Collection)

Page 141 Image 23 - *Resolution in a Gale*, by Willem Van de Velde the Younger, 1678. (National Maritime Museum, in public domain)

Page 142 Image 24 - *Stormy Sea with Sinking Ship (Dutch)*, by F J Pfeiffer (II). (Rijkmuseum)

Plates
Plate One
Daniel Defoe. Line engraving by Michael Vandergucht, after Jeremiah Taverner, 1706. (© National Portrait Gallery, London)

Plate Two
a) *Captain Robert Knox of the East India Company*. Oil on canvas by P. Trampon, 1708. (Royal Museums Greenwich, in public domain)

b) *William Dampier*. Oil on canvas by Thomas Murray, c.1697–1698. (© National Portrait Gallery, London)

c) *East Indiaman Sailing out of Marsdiep*. Oil on canvas by Hendrik Cornelisz, (between 1600 and 1630). (Rijkmuseum)

Plate Three
a) *Ships in Distress*, by Richard Bernard Godfrey, after Charles Brooking, 1796. (Yale Center for British Art, Paul Mellon Collection)

b) *Shipwrack*, by Pierre Charles Canot, after Peter Monamy. (Yale Center for British Art, Paul Mellon Collection)

Plate Four
a) *Stormy Coast Scene After a Shipwreck*. Artist unknown (French, c.1805). (Metropolitan Museum of Art)

b) *Ship on Fire at Night,* by Charles Brooking, c.1756. (Yale Center for British Art, Paul Mellon Collection)

Plate Five
a) *Ship Wrecked on a Rocky Coast*, by Charles Brooking, 1747. (Yale Center for British Art, Paul Mellon Collection)

b) *Storm Over a Coast*, by Giles F Phillips, undated. (Yale Center for British Art, Paul Mellon Collection)

Plate Six
a) *Sir Cloudesley Shovell*. Oil on canvas by Michael Dahl. (National Maritime Museum, in public domain)

b) *An English ship at Sea running in a Gale*. Oil on canvas by Willem van de Velde, the Younger, 1700. (Yale Center for British Art, Paul Mellon Collection)

c) *View of HMS* Boyne *on Fire by Accident at Spithead, 1 May 1795*. Aquatint by John William Edye. (Yale Center for British Art, Paul Mellon Collection)

Plate Seven
a) *Shipwreck Off a Rocky Coast*. Oil on canvas by Thomas Buttersworth, c.1810. (Yale Center for British Art, Paul Mellon Collection)

b) *Shipwreck*. Oil on canvas by Francis Danby, c.1850. (Yale Center for British Art, Paul Mellon Collection)

Plate Eight
a) *William Bligh* (Rear Admiral) by Alexander Huey, 1814. (National Library of Australia)

b) *William Bligh*. Pencil and watercolour by John Smart, 1803. (© National Portrait Gallery, London)

c) *Captain Bligh being forced into the longboat of HMS* Bounty, by Robert Dodd, 1796. (National Maritime Museum, in public domain)

Index